Back to the Basics: A Return to the Fundamentals of Christianity
Authored by Joyce A. Graham
Foreword by Bishop Edwin C. Bass

Library of Congress Cataloging-in-Publication Data is available upon request.

The Library of Congress
United States Copyright Office
101 Independence Ave., S.E.
Washington, D.C. 20559-6000
202-707-3000

Cover Design by Joyce A. Graham
Published by Back to the Basics Ministries

ISBN-13: 978-0692369814
ISBN-10: 0692369813
BISAC: Religion/Christian Church/Growth

Back to the Basics

Back to the Basics:

A Return to the Fundamentals of Christianity

Therefore whosoever heareth these sayings of mine, and doeth them, I will liken him unto a wise man, which built his house upon a rock: And the rain descended, and the floods came, and the winds blew, and beat upon that house; and it fell not: for it was founded upon a rock...
St. Matthew 7:24-25

Joyce A. Graham

In loving memory of…

My parents, Thomas S. Johnson and Rosa L. Johnson

My brother, Willie L. Johnson

Dedication

I dedicate this book to:

My 3 children: ***Pamela***, ***Patrice***, and ***Carl, Jr***.
My 3 granddaughters: ***Danielle***, ***Cynthia***, and ***Meghan***
My great granddaughter: ***Waverly***

Now unto Him that is able to keep you from falling, and to present you faultless before the presence of His glory with exceeding joy,

To the only wise God our Saviour, be glory and majesty, dominion and power, both now and ever. Amen.
Jude 1:24-25

Acknowledgments

I would like to acknowledge:

My husband:
Carl T. Graham, Sr.
You have shown me what love truly is...You have demonstrated that love is patient, love is kind. It does not envy, it does not boast, it is not proud. It does not dishonor others, it is not self-seeking, it is not easily angered, it keeps no record of wrongs. Love does not delight in evil but rejoices with the truth. It always protects, always trusts, always hopes, always perseveres...
1 Corinthians 13:4-7 (NIV)

My three sisters:
Myrtle L. Humphrey, ***Rosetta Watts***, and ***Dorothy J. Brown***.
Each of you in your own, unique way has modeled and epitomized what it means to be a virtuous, Godly woman. I am so blessed that you are my sisters and also my friends.

My spiritual parents:
Bishop Edwin C. Bass and ***Lady Jessie Bass***.
Thank you for always encouraging me to advance God's Kingdom with a spirit of excellence!

Foreword

By Bishop Edwin C. Bass

Joyce A. Graham's book, *Back to the Basics*, delineates the prerequisites of a successful walk with God. An understanding of this basic information is absolutely necessary to prevent Christians from living a depressing "roller coaster life" of euphoric highs and dismal lows marked by ever present fear and periodic backsliding. This book will give individuals the basic knowledge to survive and position them to gain the advanced knowledge to thrive.

Consider this example from the secular realm. More advanced forms of mathematics like algebra and geometry cannot be fully understood without first understanding basic mathematics. Basic math is essential to operating in our world for simple things like verifying the accuracy of our paychecks or buying groceries. Advanced math, however, is necessary to build skyscrapers and bridges or design cars. Honestly, one can survive in the world without algebra and geometry, but it is necessary that some in our society master advanced mathematics so that we can enjoy all that our modern society is capable of offering.

In mathematics, or any endeavor for that matter, the basics are necessary to survive and the complex is needed to thrive. Abundant blessings accrue to those who thrive. This same paradigm applies to our Christian walk. Unless we master the basics, we cannot go on to delve into the deeper truths of His Word, where the abundance of blessings is realized, because of ignorance.

This book would be a great addition to the New Convert's curriculum at any church or simply as a refresher for Christians at all stages who want a more successful walk with God or wish to assist others in achieving spiritual maturation.

Congratulations to Evangelist Joyce A. Graham for a job well done!

Bishop Edwin C. Bass
Pastor, The Empowered Church

Preface

The purpose of this book is to provoke Christians to revisit fundamental Christianity. We actually experience much of our spiritual growth from the basic fundamentals or essentials of Christianity.

Defined, a fundamental is a basic idea or foundation upon which other ideas are built. It is the common denominator—all other issues are secondary. If a fundamental is diminished, the thing it defined ceases to exist.

The list of fundamentals or essentials would definitely include Bible Study, Prayer, and Fasting. There are many others, but the principle is the same—a return to the basics is the most effective way to ensure that we are experiencing spiritual gains instead of emotional highs.

My prayer is that this book motivates, encourages, and engages you in the practice of habits and behaviors that have proven to be productive since the early days of Christianity.

In His Love,
Joyce A. Graham

Introduction

Joyce A. Graham is a gifted evangelist, teacher, and renowned author of several books and articles. In her most recent book, *Back to the Basics*, Joyce integrates insights regarding foundational truths with practical applications that are essential in the life of every believer.

Whether you have just recently begun your walk with the Lord or have been walking with Him for a number of years, this book is replete with scriptures and examples that explore Biblically based concepts such as salvation, love, forgiveness, compassion, etc.

We have an enemy who is intent on destroying the very fabric and foundation of our faith through the assault of God ordained institutions. We have witnessed the erosion of the sanctity of marriage, the dismantling of our families, and the breakdown of our communities. The rudiments and values upon which our faith was built are disintegrating before our very eyes.

Within the pages of this book, Joyce has prepared and delivered an affirming message that is highly effective in relaying and restoring those values.

Back to the Basics is a contradiction to modern day religiosity that posits that the only way we can go forward is to abandon the conventions of our predecessors. While the strategy in presenting the Gospel has changed, the original message has not.

My Personal Testimony

In April, 1973, on Easter Sunday Morning, I gave my life to the Lord. In retrospect, I had no idea that when I got up that morning, anything out of the ordinary would occur. In fact, the only reason that I was going to church at all was because my sister had invited me and it was Easter. If you know anything at all about the African-American community and culture, you know that there are two days that you attend church without fail—whether you are a Christian or not. Those two days are Easter Sunday and Mother's Day. Not attending church on those two days is considered extremely irreverent and sacrilegious.

So, after a Saturday night of drinking and clubbing, I finally made it home sometime before dawn. I slept for a few hours, then got up Sunday morning to get myself and my 9 month old baby girl ready for church. My other little girl, who was 2 years old, was at her grandma's. As I waited for my sister to pick us up, I began to dread the whole ordeal. I was not particularly anxious or excited about church. I just wanted to get it over with and get on with my life.

At the conclusion of the service, the preacher made an appeal to come forth to the altar for prayer. He went on and on, and the longer he made the appeal, the more firmly I sat in my seat. With my baby in my arms and sitting there rather defiantly, I refused to budge an inch. I remember feeling very agitated and extremely uncomfortable. Finally, he stopped and I breathed a heavy sigh of relief.

Suddenly, I looked out of the corner of my eye and saw my sister. She had gotten up from where she had been sitting and was coming toward me with her arms extended. When she reached me, she took the baby from my arms. I felt myself rising from my seat, then moving my legs one at a time until I was all the way in the front of the church. Immediately, I felt totally out of place.

Here was this skinny little black girl from Public Housing. I had just left the club the night before and I reeked of cigarettes and liquor. Besides all of that, I was dressed inappropriately. I came in wearing a micro-mini skirt, I had a huge afro, there were bracelets going up and down my arms, and I had on earring hoops the size of saucers.

Most of all, I had just come off the streets and I had issues that I knew I could not resolve on my own. But God performed a miracle! Following the instructions of the minister, I invited the Lord into my heart and received the gift of salvation that very day. Though my life has not been without challenges and struggle, I have been saved for over 40 years now. To God be the glory!

History of the Back to the Basics Ministry

The Back to the Basics Ministry began in 1986. During the 1980's, there was an explosion of technical advances. Not only could you hear the word of God on the radio, but now there were hundreds of Tele-Evangelists who had made their way to the airwaves. One day at the end of his message, a Tele-Evangelist invited his "television audience" to accept Christ. He made what is typically a simple 3-step process, into something so complicated, that at the end, one could not tell if he/she were saved or had just been invited to a barn-raising.

Somewhere along the way, preachers had begun preaching a more "Complex Gospel" than the one I heard when I first received Christ into my life. When I accepted Christ, my life was already so messed up! I had hang-ups, habits, and hurts. I needed a pure and uncomplicated Gospel. I needed someone who would give it to me straight and explain to me, "This is *how* you pray…this is *why* you fast…this is *how* you live!" I thank God for the minister who preached a simple Gospel message the day I received Christ into my life. It was that method of teaching that has served as the foundation of my faith all these years!

After hearing the Tele-Evangelist's message that day, I became concerned and deeply disturbed. From that very moment on, I purposed in my heart to find a way to reintroduce an uncomplicated Gospel and the simple plan of salvation.

God immediately directed my attention to the Gospel of **St. Matthew, Chapters 5, 6** and **7** and hence, the Back to the Basics Ministry was born!

The passages of scripture found in **St. Matthew, Chapters 5, 6,** and **7** are commonly referred to as the Sermon on the Mount. The contents of this sermon are at the very heart of the teachings of Jesus. In this sermon, Jesus lays the foundation for our salvation and not only that, but He also describes to us how to maintain our position once we have accepted Him.

Despite the many transitions that Christianity has undergone since its early days, these teachings are enduring because the contexts of these three chapters are the tenets of Christianity:

- Prayer
- Fasting
- Compassion
- Forgiveness
- Love

These are powerful scriptures to live by and though you may not have read the entire Bible from cover to cover, if you will commit to these scriptures, you will be well underway to becoming grounded in your walk with the Lord. Though simple in principle, they are extremely powerful in application. What others, (Paul, Peter, James, etc.) have written in the New Testament, actually expand upon these principles and these concepts.

Contents

Chapter 1

The Three Steps To Salvation

The Three Steps To Salvation

If thou shalt confess with thy mouth the Lord Jesus, and shalt believe in thine heart that God hath raised Him from the dead, thou shalt be Saved. For with the heart man believeth unto righteousness; and with the mouth confession is made unto Salvation. For whosoever shall call upon the name of the Lord shall be saved.
(Romans 10:9, 10 & 13)

Salvation is not complicated. In fact, receiving Christ is simple. There are only three steps to becoming saved after you have been convicted of your sins and are convinced that you are powerless over your life:

1. Confess that you are a sinner. (Acknowledge that you have sinned).

2. Repent of your sins. (You are Godly sorry and are willing to abandon all sinful behavior).

3. Receive Jesus Christ as Savior and Lord. (You relinquish all control over your life and accept Jesus as Savior and claim Him as Lord).

After you have completed those three steps, pray this simple prayer:

Father God, In the name of Jesus, I confess that I am a sinner and I come to You in prayer repenting of my sins and asking for Your forgiveness. I confess with my mouth and believe in my heart that Jesus is Your Son, and that He died on the cross at Calvary and that He rose again on the third day, that I might be forgiven and have eternal life. I invite You into my heart. Be the Lord of my life from this day forward. And now I am born again and cleansed by the Blood of Jesus! Amen

Now that you have prayed that prayer, you are saved! Your next step is to fellowship with other believers in a Bible Based Church. Welcome to God's Family!

Chapter 2

How Important is the Foundation of My Faith?

How Important is the Foundation of My Faith?

Therefore, whosoever heareth these sayings of mine, and doeth them, I will liken him unto a wise man, which built his house upon a rock; And the rain descended, and the floods came, and the winds blew, and beat upon that house; and it fell not for it was founded upon a rock.

And everyone that heareth these sayings of mine and doeth them not, shall be likened unto a foolish man, which built his house upon the sand; And the rain descended, and the floods came, and the winds blew, and beat upon that house; and it fell, and great was the fall of it.
(St. Matthew 7:24-27)

In these passages of scripture, Jesus makes a very sobering contrast between two builders and two foundations. Their experience is somewhat similar:

- They both had building material for houses.
- They both built their houses.
- At the end of construction, both houses were standing.

However, somewhere in the process, one of the builders took a short-cut. This builder, no doubt, completed his house days, weeks, maybe even months before the other builder. But, because the house was built on sand, it had no depth, no stability, and no durability.

If we are not careful, the enemy will trick us into believing that we can take short-cuts. Lose 20 pounds in 7 days! Give me 2 weeks and I'll show you how to become a millionaire! 3 days to a miracle! Drink this! Swallow that! Go here! Go there! Precious people of the Lord, there are no *short-cuts*. Anything worthwhile and lasting is labor intensive.

The other builder dug deep into the ground until he hit bedrock and only then did he proceed to build his house. Though undetected from the appearance of the exterior, the houses were polar opposites in terms of foundation and support.

The Bible says that the rain descended, and the floods came, and the winds blew and beat upon both houses. The house that was built upon sand fell. Why? Not necessarily because of the severity of the storm—the storm was identical! It fell simply because the foundation could not support it. The house that was built on a solid foundation or rock withstood the storm, and the Bible says that it fell not because it was built upon a rock.

What are the spiritual implications of this parable? Without a solid foundation, we will have a similar fate as the house in the parable that was built upon sand. However, if we build on a rock or on a solid foundation, we will endure the storms of life. Metaphorically, that rock or that solid foundation is simply the Word of God!

What causes one person to stand and another to fall? What causes one person to throw in the towel and another to overcome? What causes one person to succumb and another to endure? The answer is obedience to the Word of God!

We must have more than our logic, our intellect, or our will to make it. Our minds have betrayed us before; our wills have derailed us more than once; even our own bodies have let us down! So we cannot trust our emotions or our feelings, bccause as someone once said, "Sometimes I feel like a nut—sometimes I don't!" We have got to have something that is bedrock solid, and I know of no other thing on this earth that is more stable than the Word of God!

Chapter 3

Who Am I Now?

Who Am I Now?

Therefore if any man be in Christ, he is a new creature: old things are passed away; behold, all things are become new.
(II Corinthians 5:17)

Everyone experiences existential issues, whether the source is of an internal or external origin. We are born with almost an insatiable desire and an obsession for a meaningful existence. After we are saved, that quest for meaning intensifies. It is further fueled by our desire to know what our position, purpose, and destiny is in the Kingdom of God.

In **St. Matthew 16:13-15**, Jesus asked His disciples, *"Whom do men say that I the Son of man am?" And they answered, "Some say that thou art John the Baptist, some, Elias, and others, Jeremias, or one of the prophets." He saith unto them, "But whom say ye that I am?"*

Jesus did not ask this question because He was conflicted or confused about His identity. He knew that He was the Son of God. But He also knew that there were questions that centered around His authenticity and acclaim to being the Son of God. There were preconceived ideas and even misconceptions as to the purpose His coming would serve and the manner in which He would fulfill and accomplish that purpose. He was keenly aware that He did not meet the expectations of the people.

In **St. Matthew 11:3**, John asked, *"Art thou He that should come, or do we look for another?"* Interestingly, Jesus did not validate John's question with explanations or verifications concerning His identity. Instead, He responded with evidence of what *God* was doing *through* Him: the blind received their sight, the lame walked, the lepers were cleansed, the deaf heard again, the dead were raised, and the Gospel was preached to the poor. This substantiates the fact that the essence of who we are is intricately linked to the manifestation of God working through us and our willingness in allowing Him to do so. It is then, and only then, that our existence is solidified.

Jesus was called a liar, a drunkard, and was even accused of being in league with the devil. He never internalized those accusations. Jesus is our perfect example as to how we should respond when our salvation, our identity, or our purpose is questioned by others. Just as He was totally and completely affirmed by God, we must also realize that it is God who defines and validates our very existence; not people, not our past, not our failures, trials, or circumstances. More importantly, our self-image and self-worth cannot ever be based on our own perception of ourselves.

There is a widely accepted theory that alleges that traumatic experiences of our childhood forever shape our lives after we become adults. When I reflect on my own childhood trauma, I now realize that my view of myself was extremely distorted before coming to the Lord. I was a victim of childhood abuse at the hands of people who were considered trusted friends of my family. Those experiences were wrong at the time that they were committed, but, being a child, I could not interpret the acts themselves as being appropriate or inappropriate, good or bad. Neither could I separate the acts from me, the child. So I internalized them and allowed those experiences to affect my self-image. Now that I am saved and an adult, I can interpret them through the eyes of God. Though the acts were wrong and inappropriate, they do not define who I am now!

We must never struggle with trying to live out how other people perceive us. We must not adapt to another's perception of us and adopt that perception as our own. And we must not be constrained nor limited by our own inabilities. Our self-worth is not predicated on anything other than this one statement: I am who God says I am! [1]

Chapter 4

What Shall I Do With Jesus, Who Is Called Christ?

What Shall I Do With Jesus, Who Is Called Christ?

The governor answered and said unto them, "Whether of the twain will ye that I release unto you?" They said, "Barabbas."

Pilate saith unto them, "What shall I do then with Jesus which is called Christ?" They all say unto him, "Let Him be crucified." ***(St. Matthew 27:21-22)***

In **St. Matthew, Chapter 26**, the writer lays the foundation of the events leading up to the crucifixion of Jesus. Several years ago, there was a movie entitled *"The Passion of the Christ,"* which very graphically and with great accuracy depicted the physical suffering of our Lord.[2] During the viewing in which I was present, people were literally weeping as we sat and watched the depiction of Christ being beaten and then the spikes driven through His wrists and through His ankles.

When Jesus was here on earth in the flesh, He was essentially just like you and me in terms of being triune; that is spirit, soul and body. Otherwise, how could He relate to us? The Bible says in the book of **Hebrews 2:16-18**, that *"He took not on Him the nature of angels, but He took on Him the seed of Abraham. Wherefore in all things it behooved Him to be made like unto His bretheren that He* *might be a merciful and faithful high priest in things pertaining to God, to make reconciliation for the sins of the people. For in that He Himself hath suffered being tempted, He is able to succour them that are tempted."* That word "succour" simply means "help." He is able to help us because He can identify with us on a spiritual, emotional, and physical level.

There were also spiritual and emotional ramifications associated with the death of Jesus because He had an emotional as well as a spiritual connection to God. So what were the emotional and spiritual aspects of Calvary?

We know that in the garden of Gethsemane, Jesus said, *"My soul is exceeding sorrowful, even unto death."* Meaning that He was grieved and that He struggled emotionally with the decision to follow through with the assignment of Calvary. It was during this time that He prayed for the cup to pass from Him—the cup of sin. But Jesus understood that enduring Calvary was the only way that He could be presented as the icon of sin without committing sin Himself.

What about the spiritual ramifications? There was a space in time where the Father had to turn away from Him because of the sin He bore. The spiritual connection that He had with God all of His existence was temporarily severed. Think of it!

Every one of us should ask the same question that Pilate raised to the Mob; *"What shall I do with Jesus who is called Christ?"* Because if His death and His resurrection have not impacted every one of us on a personal level, then His dying and His resurrection were in vain.

We tend to be very critical of the mob that shouted, *"Crucify Him!"* We say that if we were there and living in that day, we would never be a part of that mob. But when we reject Christ, we are saying, "Crucify Him!" Maybe not audibly, but we imply it when we reject Him.

For those of us who accepted Him at one time and then make a conscious decision to walk away, **Hebrews 6:6** defines it as *"Crucifying Him afresh, and putting Him to an open shame."*

But there is still hope! Job asked the question, in the book of **Job 14:14**, *"If a man die, shall he live again?"* Jesus is the answer to that question. The answer is a resounding *yes*. There is hope, for death no longer represents the end. The sting has been taken out of death and the grave and both are swallowed up in victory!

Romans 4:25 says that *"Jesus was delivered for our offences, and was raised again for our justification."* The Amplified version of that same passage says that *"Jesus was betrayed and put to death because of our misdeeds and was raised to secure our justification or* *our acquittal making our account balance and absolving us from all guilt before God."* This scripture encapsulates why Jesus died and why He rose again. Praise God!

Every one of us must asked ourselves the same question that Pilate raised to the crowd, *"What shall I do with Jesus who is called Christ?"*

Chapter 5

What Purpose Does the Pastor Serve in My Life?

What Purpose Does the Pastor Serve in My Life?

And I will give you Pastors according to mine heart, which shall feed you with knowledge and understanding.
(Jeremiah 3:15)

The duties of the watchman in biblical times were to alert the townspeople of climatic changes in the atmosphere, broadcast the time according to the alignment of the sun, moon, and stars, and warn the townspeople of approaching danger. His physical position, high in the watchtower, allowed great visibility. From this vantage point, he could observe activity occurring in the city and the surrounding areas at a glance.

Because the safety of the entire town depended upon him, the selection process of the watchman was conducted very meticulously and with much deliberation. His ability to detect adverse conditions, demonstrate unconditional love regardless of his own personal relationships, and pledge total dedication to the well being of the townspeople was paramount. The watchman had the sole responsibility of sounding the alarm at the slightest hint of danger. Therefore, he had to be on duty at all times; putting the safety of others above his own.

As the townspeople slept safely in their beds, the watchman stayed awake, keeping vigil over the entire city. Whenever anyone felt threatened, anxious, or needed to be reassured regarding the status of their safety, they would look up to the watchtower and inquire, *"Watchman, what of the night?"*[3] The watchman would give the report that danger was lurking or that all was well.

In the book of **Isaiah, Chapter 21**, the Bible gives an account of a watchman's detection of approaching danger. Far in the distance, he observed the enemy with dust rising from the wheels of the war chariots and he heard the beat of the horses' hooves. The watchman immediately sounded the alarm and cried, *"...here cometh a chariot of men!"*

Although the news was disconcerting, the early warning provided an opportunity for the people to arm themselves for war, prepare to fight, and, most importantly, repent of their sins if need be.

The report that particular night was grim and disturbing indeed. As the townspeople prepared for the worse, God inspired the watchman to broadcast an additional message. This time, the message was one of hope. The watchman cried out the second time and said, *"The morning cometh!"* This signaled to the people that God had not forsaken them; that after the night had ended, dawn would break bringing hope and encouragement with the new day!

God has commissioned and charged modern day watchmen with an identical task. He has adorned these watchmen with spiritual eyes, enabling them to see what the natural eye cannot see; and a discerning spirit, enabling them to detect what the natural senses cannot detect. They are to warn His people of approaching danger, but just as the example above illustrated, that message must be coupled with a message of hope. A watchman cannot discharge his duties with any great level of precision if he omits either message.

It is a privilege to have watchmen assigned to us in the person of Pastors. God has ordained and anointed them to watch over our souls, correct us when we are in error, console us when it is darkest in our lives, warn us of imminent danger, and encourage us when it seems all hope is gone.

All of us have experienced a time when life was as dark as a thousand midnights. All of us have had "nighttime" descend upon us seemingly without warning. Nighttime came when we had a pressing burden and we needed our Pastor to pray for us.

Nighttime came when we or a loved one fell gravely ill and we summoned our Pastor to our hospital bed or to the bedside of the sick loved one. Nighttime came when our child had gone astray and our Pastor ministered to him/her. In each of those instances and in others, we were inquiring of our Pastor, *"Watchman, what of the night?"* And the watchman replied with the voice of faith, hope, and encouragement, *"The morning cometh!"* What blessed assurance to know that the watchman is "on the wall!"

Chapter 6

What If I Am Still Struggling?

What If I Am Still Struggling?

I find then a law, that, when I would do good, evil is present with me. For I delight in the law of God after the inward man: But I see another law in my members, warring against the law of my mind, and bringing me into captivity to the law of sin which is in my members. O wretched man that I am! Who shall deliver me from the body of this death?
(Romans 7:21-24)

There is an old Native American Folklore about a grandfather who was teaching his young grandson about the struggles of life.[4] He said to his grandson, "There is a terrible fight going on inside of me. It is between two wolves. One wolf represents fear, anger, envy, sorrow, regret, greed, arrogance, self-pity, guilt, resentment, inferiority, lies, false pride, superiority, and ego. The other wolf represents joy, peace, love, hope, sharing, serenity, humility, kindness, benevolence, friendship, empathy, generosity, truth, compassion, and faith."

The grandfather continued, "This same fight is going on inside of you, and inside every other person in the world."

The grandson thought about it for a minute and then asked his grandfather, "Which wolf will win?"

The old grandfather simply replied, "The one you feed."

We can apply this same analogy to our Christian experience. Paul very passionately describes this internal struggle in **Romans 7:21-24**: *"I find then a law, that, when I would do good, evil is present with me. For I delight in the law of God after the inward man: But I see another law in my members, warring against the law of my mind, and bringing me into captivity to the law of sin which is in my members. O wretched man that I am! Who shall deliver me from the body of this death?"*

Paul alluded to the fact that the Christian walk is not an event; it is an ongoing process involving deliberate and informed decision making. We must first realize and accept, as Paul did, that we are engaged in an internal battle; a power struggle of good vs. evil. We must diligently seek the counsel of God which is tantamount to our choosing wisely. Then continue in the quest of embracing doctrinal truths and releasing erroneous concepts; of adopting behavior that will result in the reaping of eternal rewards and avoiding behavior that will result in negative consequences; of attaining spiritual gains and rejecting short-lived emotional highs.

Paul also said in **Romans 6:16 & 19b**, *"Know ye not, that to whom ye yield yourselves servants to obey, his servants ye are to whom ye obey; whether of sin unto death, or of obedience unto righteousness? For as ye have yielded your members servants to* *uncleaness and to iniquity unto iniquity; even so now yield your members servants to righteousness unto holiness."*

The old grandfather was simply telling his grandson that whichever wolf is fed, he is the one who receives strength, and eventually emerges as the dominant one. If we nurture and sustain the good and starve and deprive the evil, in the end, we will experience triumphant victory. Which wolf will you feed?

Chapter 7

Spiritual Maturity

Spiritual Maturity

But grow in grace, and in the knowledge of our Lord and Saviour Jesus Christ. To him be glory both now and forever. Amen.
(2 Peter 3:18)

Spiritual Maturity is crucial in the life of every believer. Growth is one of the demands that God places on every living thing. Babies are expected to thrive, to grow, and to develop into healthy adults.

I have a granddaughter named Meghan. Meghan was approaching 4 years old and the time for Meghan to get rid of her pacifier had come and gone. Her mother knew it, I knew it, and I suspect that even Meghan knew it.

It had gotten to the point of being so ridiculous, that Meghan would snatch the pacifier out of her mouth whenever she was around her little friends or whenever we were going on an outing.

One day Meghan came to spend the weekend with me as she often does and her mother had forgotten to pack the pacifier. I panicked and called her Mother and said, “What are we going to do, we have no pacifier!” When bedtime came, Meghan demanded her pacifier. Well, I realized that I didn’t have one at the house, so I started putting on my clothes to go out into the dead of the night to find one.

When I thought about how ridiculous the whole thing was, I stopped abruptly, sat down, and called Meghan to me. I said, "Meghan you are not a baby anymore and you need to say goodbye to your pacifier. You are a big girl now and you can fall asleep without the pacifier." To my surprise, Meghan said, "OK, Nanny." And she has not had one since.

What Meghan did and what we all must do is grow up. Paul said in **1 Corinthians, 13:11**, *"When I was a child, I spake as a child, I understood as a child, I thought as a child: but when I became a man, I put away childish things."*

Growth is also an expectation of all life form. Underdeveloped animals are called the runt of the litter and are of little value. Fishermen throw the smaller fish back into the pond. Plants that fail to thrive and produce, after a while, are uprooted or cut down.

Remember the parable of the fig tree? The book of **St. Luke Chapter 13, 6-7**, gives an account of a certain man who had a fig tree planted in his vineyard, and he came and sought fruit thereon, and found none. Then said he unto the dresser of his vineyard, *"Behold these three years I come seeking fruit on this fig tree, and find none. Cut it down!"* The Amplified version of the same verse says, *"Why should it continue to use up the ground, deplete the soil, intercept the sun, and take up room?"*

When Jesus was hungry, the Bible says in **St. Matthew 21:19**, *"He saw a fig tree in the way, came to it, and found nothing thereon, but leaves only, and said unto it, 'Let no fruit grow on thee hence forward forever.' And presently the fig tree withered away."*

Why? The fig tree failed to produce. It failed to develop. It failed to thrive. And my concern is that in the church, we have people who are failing to progress spiritually. In a day and in a time when we are inundated with the Word of God, why is there so much spiritual immaturity in the church? And as a process of elimination, we have to come to the conclusion that spiritual maturity is not what we think it is. It has nothing to do with our longevity as Christians. It is not predicated on how much knowledge of scripture we have acquired. And it is definitely not related to how well we can pull a sermon together.

But it has everything to do with how we apply God's word to our lives, how we walk in obedience to Him, and how we allow the Holy Spirit to govern our behavior.

So how do we define spiritual maturity and what does it look like?

Spiritual maturity is an ongoing process of growth that begins when a person accepts Jesus Christ as Savior. There are:

1. Conditions for growth
2. Steps to growth
3. Evidence of growth

Let's begin with conditions for growth: I have indentified 3 conditions for growth. They are:

1. Planting
2. Nurturing
3. Pruning

How can we grow if we have not been planted or we have no sense of stability? By that I mean that we do not stay anywhere long enough to get rooted and grounded in the Word of God. Some of us go from one church to the other and we have not established any roots. Paul said in the book of **Ephesians 4:14**, that we are to be *"No more children, who are tossed to and fro, and carried about with every wind of doctrine, by the sleight of men, and cunning craftiness, whereby they lie in wait to deceive."*

If you are a church drifter, you are getting your spiritual food on the run. You are eating from *this* table and from *that* table and after awhile, your spiritual system becomes irregular. Then you become vulnerable because you have no stability. Yes, there is a church on almost every corner in almost every city, but we needn't feel obligated to sample each one.

We must also be nurtured. Just as plants must have both sunshine and rain, we must have all of the necessary nutrients for spiritual maturity. Messages of prosperity are fine, messages of motivation are fine, messages admonishing us to praise God are fine and they all have their place, but we need the rain, too. We must be challenged and we must be stretched in order to grow.

Finally, we must be pruned. The pruning process is uncomfortable because it involves extractions. As we grow to maturity, there are behaviors that we must eliminate, strongholds that must be broken, and even thought processes that must be redirected.

Paul says it best in the book of **Hebrews 6:1-2**, *"Therefore leaving the principles of the doctrine of Christ, let us go on unto perfection, not laying again the foundation of repentance from dead works, and of faith toward God, of the doctrine of baptisms, and of laying of hands, and of resurrection of the dead, and of eternal judgment."*

What Paul is saying is that there is a level of progression. There are some things that we should be beyond. When he talks about perfection, he is simply talking about maturity. Simply stated, we should not be stumbling over what we stumbled over 5 years ago. Ask yourself the following question: Am I repenting over and over again for the same old sin? If you and I do some honest reflecting, we will realize that God has another level and another dimension for us. It is time for us to confront and conquer whatever it is that is stunting our growth in Christ.

Just as there are conditions for growth, there are also steps to growth: They are:

1. We must desire to grow
2. We must be obedient
3. We must do the essentials

We must first have a desire to grow. **I Peter 2:2** admonishes us to *"Desire the sincere milk of the word, that we may grow thereby."* When Peter said that we are to grow in grace and in the knowledge of our Lord and Savior Jesus Christ, he was not talking about intellectual knowledge. Peter was talking about a full knowledge of Jesus; an increasing awareness of what we have after having come to Him and the capacity and the ability to expand upon it. God never advocates lack in any area of our lives.

In the absence of a desire to grow, we lack ambition and we lack motivation in the things of God. We become like the servants in whom the Lord invested, and upon returning and making an assessment, found that the one servant had not progressed at all. This greatly displeased the Lord.

Our steps to growth must certainly include obedience to the Word of God. That is we must not only hear the word, but we must walk in obedience to that word. In the Old Testament, the Hebrew word translated into English as obedience means "to hear."

The New Testament expands on this and gets even more detailed. In the Greek, the word obedience means "to hear or listen in a state of submission" or "attentive hearkening." The operative word in that definition is hearkening. How many of you know that hearing from the Lord and doing what you have heard are not synonymous? Hearing does not equate to doing.

All of us can look back to a time where we walked in disobedience, even after having accepted the Lord into our hearts and into our lives. Those times when doing it our way looked more appealing than doing it God's way. And I think that we sometimes feel as though we have gotten away with disobedience because we aren't walking around with a lightning bolt through our foreheads.

However, just because we don't see physical evidence of discipline right away, does not mean that it is not forthcoming. God would much rather show mercy. However, there are always consequences to disobedience. And though we may not link our disobedience to some of the adversity in our lives, if we do some honest reflection, we will see what that wrong decision cost us.

Many of us are just now recovering from situations that are a direct result of our disobedience. There will never be a time in our lives that we have to step *outside* of God's will to get anything. Neither can we "get over" on God or outmaneuver Him. God has established precepts, laws and principles of conduct for us for our own good. And those laws are universal. It does not matter if we go to the other side of the planet and do what we want to do, God sees it.

How much further along would some of us be right now if we had just trusted God and went on and did it His way? We must realize that we are limited as humans, and oftentimes, we have tunnel vision and cannot see the big picture. However, God has panoramic vision and He sees how *this* will affect *that* and what we consider the scenic route will end in disaster.

God views disobedience as a form of betrayal. As much as God loved David and as much as David loved God, when David sinned with Bathsheba, God said to him, *"Why have you despised my commandment and done evil in my sight? I anointed you king over Israel, I delivered you out of the hand of Saul, I gave you your master's house, I even gave you their wives, and I gave you the house of Israel and of Judah, And if that had been too little, I would moreover have given unto you such and such things."*

Obedience requires trust. **Proverbs 3:5 & 6** encourages us to *"Trust in the Lord with all thine heart and lean not unto thine own understanding. In all thy ways acknowledge Him and He shall direct thy paths."*

And finally in our steps to growth, we must do the essentials. What are the essentials? We must study the Word of God, we must pray, and we must fast. Those three essentials are grass-root Christianity. They are basic and fundamental and are the staples of our success as people of the Lord.

How can we know what God's instructions are to us and how will we know what He has to say about the affairs of our lives if we do not study His word? The Bible says that we are to *"Study to show thyself approved unto God, a workman that needeth not be ashamed rightly dividing the word of truth."*

In his book entitled, "*The Importance of God's Word*," David Humpal wrote: [5]

> *We learn about the Lord's mercy and love to us from the Psalms, and we learn about God's judgment and righteousness from the Prophets. We find out about God's long-suffering and patience with us from the Gospels, and we learn about His anger against sin from the Books of Moses. We read about God reaching out to save the Gentiles in the Book of Acts, and we read about God judging the Gentile nations in the Book of Revelation.*

> *We see One who keeps the world spinning and yet still has time for our smallest problems. We learn of the One who is moving nations and yet still has time for our family. We find out about the One who has the vast physical realm of the entire universe under His control, and yet He still has time for our physical problems. We meet the One whose intellect is so far superior to us that we can barely understand how all His creation functions, and yet He still has time for us when we are suffering mental anguish.*

Prayer is another essential. *(Please refer to Chapter 18 on Prayer).* We must communicate and seek the counsel of God daily, so we must have a consistent prayer life. Prayer is one of those things that a lot of people have made so complex, when it is simply communing with God. It is nothing more and nothing less than that.

Fasting is also an essential. *(Please refer to Chapter 19 on Fasting).* Fasting brings the flesh under subjection and it also causes a heightened spiritual awareness.

Finally there should be evidence of growth. How do we know that we are growing? How do we know that we have progressed and are better than we were, say a year before? How can we measure spiritual maturity? Everyone one of us is to examine ourselves and see where we are and the measuring rod is not one another, but the measuring rod is Jesus. How do we measure up when we stand beside Him? In **Galatians 5**, scripture encourages us to look within ourselves for the evidence of spiritual maturity by the fruit of the spirit; love, joy, peace, longsuffering, gentleness, goodness, faith, meekness, and temperance which is self-control.

As we examine ourselves and take spiritual inventory, which is something that we should all be doing on a regular basis, we should see these attributes increasing in greater measure.

Jesus spoke of another indicator of spiritual maturity. In **St. Matthew 20:26-27**, He said that spiritual greatness is measured by servant-hood. *"Whosoever will be great among you, let him be your minister. And whosoever will be chief among you, let him be your servant."*

The higher we advance spiritually, the greater capacity we will have as servants because spiritual advancement and spiritual progression is ultimately not for us, but it is for the people of the Lord and for the advancement of the Kingdom of God.

In **2 Peter 1:5-8**, Peter admonishes us to *"Give all diligence to add to your faith virtue, and to virtue knowledge and to knowledge temperance, and to temperance patience, and to patience Godliness, and to Godliness brotherly kindness, and to brotherly kindness charity [which is love]. For if these things be in you, and abound, they make you that ye shall neither be barren nor unfruitful in the knowledge of our Lord Jesus Christ."*

Our spiritual growth is incremental and we grow in increments, but we should never be stagnant. We never reach a spiritual plateau where we just sort of level off. In the book of **Hebrews 6:1**, Paul admonishes us to, *"Leave the principles of the doctrine of Christ, and go on unto perfection; not laying again the foundation of repentance from dead works, and of faith toward God."* What Paul is saying is that we must get beyond the elementary stages in the teaching and doctrine of Christ and advance to spiritual maturity.

Pastors spend a great deal of time and effort on people who don't have a desire to grow up. People who want to stay babies because babies take no responsibility for their spiritual growth and they just simply ride. So when Pastors have to take time to "lay again the foundation of repentance from what should be dead works," it takes away from promoting the spiritual growth of the other believers. They have to pet, and stroke, and tip around some of us because we cannot handle meat.

Paul said it best in **Hebrews 5:12** when he said, *"For when the time ye ought to be teachers, ye have need that one teach you again which be the first principles of the oracles of God; and are become such as have need of milk, and not of strong meat."*

God is calling for every man, woman, boy and girl who is professing salvation to "*grow up*!"

Chapter 8

The Pit Stop

The Pit Stop

Not that I speak in respect of want: for I have learned, in whatsoever state I am, therewith to be content. I know both how to be abased, and I know how to abound: everywhere and in all things I am instructed both to be full and to be hungry, both to abound and to suffer need. I can do all things through Christ which strengtheneth me!
(Philippians 4:11-13)

In the above passage of scripture, Paul talks about two very basic fundamental concepts of life. If we are ever going to survive life at all, wc must embrace these two concepts:

1. We must learn how to adjust
2. We must learn how to adapt

We are on our way to heaven; but for now, you and I must live down here on earth. So we must be able to make our adjustments and adapt to what has changed.

I was recently hospitalized for a condition that broadsided me, seemingly, from out of nowhere. The doctors in the Emergency Room could not identify the cause of my condition, but presented several diagnostic theories. Each diagnosis seemed worse than the one before.

After I was admitted to my room, I became very concerned because the tests that they were contemplating were very invasive. For those of you who have ever been in the hospital, you know how it feels—it seems as though you are never going to see the light of day ever again. So up until this point, I did not have an official diagnosis nor a definite course of treatment; just a lot of innuendo.

I went through all of the "religious calisthenics" while waiting in my room. I talked to God, I rebuked the devil, and I looked in the mirror and decreed healing to myself.

When I finally settled in and actually listened to the Lord, He said to me, "This is just a pit stop." I asked God, "What does that mean?"

The Lord reminded me that during long car races, the cars often make what are called "pit stops." Typically, the car leaves the main race track and goes to a side lane. Located in the side lane is an area where the car is refueled, has its tires checked, etc. The primary goal of the pit stop is to make the adjustments the car needs so that it can return to the race as quickly as possible.

God repeated to me "This is just a pit stop."

I then began to relax because after God had spoken to me, I realized that this situation was not permanent. Where I had envisioned weeks in the hospital, having to undergo several invasive procedures, and examined all of the what if scenarios, God clearly assured me that my condition was only *temporary*.

It turned out to be a matter of the doctors making some simple adjustments to my medications; one was discontinued, one that I had stopped taking was resumed, and a new one was added. After the adjustments, all of my vitals were back to normal.

So what is a pit stop in life? A pit stop is a place of interruption where life as we know it is disrupted. It is only a temporary location. Put in proper perspective, it is the place that may very well propel us toward the destiny that God has for our lives. We are not to set up permanent housing at the pit stop; we are not to hang curtains; we are not to put out the welcome door mat. We are not going to live there; it is a temporary pit stop!

Joseph had to make a pit stop on his way to the palace. You and I have the luxury of turning to the end of Joseph's story, so we know that the pit was neither his destiny nor his destination. We know that the pit was not a permanent location for him.

But Joseph didn't know that! All Joseph knew was that he was stripped of his coat of many colors, thrown into a pit, and sold into slavery. What probably caused further confusion for Joseph was that it was his brothers who threw him into the pit!

However, there was a clue in the pit! The Bible says in **Genesis 37:24**, *"And they took him, and cast him into a pit; and the pit was empty, there was no water in it."*

Now here is the clue. Since the Bible specifically states that there was no water in the pit, we can assume that the pit was not a place that would sustain life. Therefore it was a temporary place and a temporary situation!

Once you and I have endured and survived the pit, we are ready to emerge from the pit and get back in this race we call life. We must make those adjustments, adapt to those changes, and continue our journey to the palace.

Embrace that dream of being the supervisor while you are yet in the mailroom! Embrace that dream of building a beautiful edifice while you are yet in the storefront! Embrace that dream of owning a home while you are yet in the shack! There is life after the pit!

Chapter 9

The Principle of Sowing and Reaping

The Principle of Sowing and Reaping

And let us not be weary in well doing: for in due season we shall reap, if we faint not.
(Galatians 6:9)

Sowing and reaping is a law and a principle instituted by God that even God, Himself, never violates. God established this principle right after the flood in **Genesis 8:22** when He said, *"While the earth remaineth, seedtime and harvest, cold and heat, summer and winter, day and night shall not cease."*

This principle operates both in the natural and in the spiritual realm. When a farmer sows a seed in the natural, he expects that seed to reproduce and return a harvest. When we sow seeds in the spiritual realm, we can also expect those seeds to reproduce and return a harvest.

The scripture in **Galatians 6:9** talks about something called *"due season."* What exactly is due season? In the example of the farmer who sows a seed, due season is a point in time that comes after the seed has germinated deep within the earth, sprouts, pushes its way up through the surface of the ground, and then bears fruit. The end of this whole process is called due season.

In the spiritual realm, due season is also the end of a process. It is after we have sown the seed, the seed representing our effort or labor or any kind of spiritual investment we make, whether it is in a relationship, our ministry, or our spiritual vocation. Those seeds will go through a similar process of germination, sprouting, and finally manifesting themselves in the bearing of fruit.

The Amplified version of **Galatians 6:9** says, *"And let us not lose heart and grow weary and faint in acting nobly and doing right, for in due time and at the appointed season we shall reap, if we do not loosen and relax our courage and faint."* What we sow goes through a kind of metamorphosis. If we don't lose heart during the process, then we will reap.

Many times, we are not aware of just how close we are to reaping our victory or obtaining our harvest because we do not know where we are in the process. However, all we are responsible for is the sowing and the reaping; *and not the process.* After the seed that we have sown leaves our hand, it is God's responsibility that we reap in kind.

We may be at the point of breaking the metaphorical surface of the earth, but if we aren't careful, we may abort the mission too soon because we become weary and tired.

I am reminded of a young lady who married a young man from Africa. This young man came to the United States as a child and as far as he was concerned, the United States was his home. Shortly after they were married, it was discovered that there was a problem in the authenticity of his citizenship documents. The government ordered him to return to Africa because for some reason, his residency in the United States was not considered legal.

This resulted in that young couple being separated very early in their marriage. While her husband was deported back to Africa, the young lady did everything that was within her power to resolve this. Naturally she was praying and everyone who was aware of this situation was praying with her. She finally contacted the Department of Immigration, the Department of Naturalization, and had even hired a lawyer, all to no avail.

This went on for several years and being a very young lady and newly married, this situation began to take its toll on her, as you can well imagine. The couple had purchased a house just before her husband left, so there were also financial concerns.

One day, the young lady and I were talking. I noticed that she did not sound as optimistic about the prospect of her husband returning as she had in the past. So, on this particular day, she was being very transparent and just speaking from her heart—she was being real with me that day.

She confided that she was tired and didn't know if her husband was ever coming back. She admitted that she didn't know how much more she could take, and contemplated aloud that maybe she should just give up. I opened my mouth to tell her that I knew how she felt; that she was only human.

However, when I opened my big old mouth to say those things to her, the Holy Spirit seemed to take control of my words and I heard myself say, "Why don't you give God a chance to work this out for you." She reluctantly agreed and within a few weeks, her husband was back in the States!

In retrospect, what she didn't know and what I didn't know is where, exactly, she was in the process! But God knew! And all God needed was a vessel so that the Holy Spirit could minister to her!

There are some of us who have invested heavily in a relationship; poured our life's blood into a church; given all we had to a career. It appears that our labor is in vain.

1 Corinthians 15:58 admonishes us to *"Be ye stedfast, unmoveable, always abounding in the work of the Lord, forasmuch as ye know that your labor is not in vain in the Lord."* Our harvest might not come from the source of our investment, but since God himself has instituted this seedtime and harvest principle, it is totally foolproof!

Chapter 10

How to Obtain and Maintain the Victory!

How to Obtain and Maintain the Victory!

So shall they fear the name of the Lord from the west, and His glory from the rising of the sun. When the enemy shall come in like a flood the spirit of the Lord shall lift up a standard against him.
(Isaiah 59:19)

The thief cometh not but for to steal and to kill and to destroy. I am come that they might have and life and that they might have it more abundantly.
(St. John 10:10)

Submit yourselves therefore to God. Resist the devil and he will flee from you.
(James 4:7)

When we look at these three passages of scripture, two common themes emerge right away:

1. God intends for us to obtain the victory in our lives.
2. God intends for us to maintain the victory in our lives.

Those two facts are constant and always have and always will be true. Victory from God's perspective is not temporary. When God gives us the victory and when we conquer a thing, in God's mind it is to be permanent. So we've established that God intends for us to live victoriously. However, the problem that I have observed in my own life and you have probably observed this in your lives as well, is that as soon as we realize victory, the enemy is always present to attempt to take that victory from us. So the issue is not so much as getting the victory or obtaining the blessing; we experience a level of victory in our lives on a regular basis. The issue is maintaining the victory.

Have you ever noticed that as soon as you go to the next level; as soon as you gain ground; as soon as you are productive; as soon as you are successful, here comes the enemy? Almost immediately, sometimes! So how do we maintain the victory?

Well first, let's talk about how we lose it. We lose it in one of two ways:

1. We either relinquish it; that is we freely give it up.
2. We allow the enemy to steal it from us.

Think about how the business world operates. I have worked in educational settings most of my life. One of the strategies that they employ is called "Recruitment and Retention."

Colleges initiate their recruitment and retention efforts at the very same exact time. They realize that it is not enough to attract students to the campus and it is not enough to get students to enroll. They want those students to come back! Therein lies the secret: Since they deploy both of these strategies simultaneously, the students come back!

This principle is nothing new. It is a principle instituted by God. All throughout the Bible; when God blessed *anybody* with *anything*, He also told them how to keep it.

When God blessed Solomon with wisdom and riches, God instructed him as to how to maintain it at the very same time. When God placed Adam and Eve in the garden, God established boundaries by informing them that Paradise was the place for their enjoyment, but in order for them to remain there, they must not eat from a certain tree. When they disobeyed, they had to leave. And when God finally brought the Children of Israel into the land flowing with milk and honey, He instructed them how to keep their land. He informed them not to allow anyone to coexist with them except the people who He designated, warning them that if they disobeyed, those people would prove to be a snare and a stumbling block.

James 4:7 admonishes us to submit ourselves to God, but to also resist the devil and he would flee from us. However, resistance is not a passive concept. We do not wait until the enemy gets there, because we know that he is coming. Before we even see him coming, we must begin our resistance strategy.

From a natural perspective, we do not wait until the thief attempts to break into our homes before we install a lock on the door. We install the lock and then we lock our doors *before* the attempt is made. We also arm our cars with burglar alarm systems before any attempt is made to vandalize them. We must arm ourselves to counter the attack of the enemy before he comes in that same manner.

The lyrics of a popular song says, “I went to the enemy’s camp and I took back what he stole from me.” These lyrics beg an answer to the following three questions:

1. Why are we allowing the enemy to get all the way back to his camp with our stuff?
2. Isn’t there something that we should be doing somewhere in that process of him coming to our camp, taking our stuff, and then making it all the way back to his camp?
3. At the very least, shouldn’t there be some signs of resistance on our part?

Figuratively speaking, the enemy should have heel marks on the back of his head, scratch marks on his back, *something* indicative of the fact that there was some resistance on our part and that he didn’t just waltz off to his camp with our stuff!

Resistance is not passive, it is aggressive! **Ephesians 6:11-18** instructs us to put on the whole amour of God and the majority of those weapons are not defensive, but they are *offensive*.

It is time out for this laying down, caving in, and taking a dive! It is not God's will for you and me to be up and down; back and forth. First I have it and it's mine. Then the enemy comes and takes it all the way back to his camp. Then I run and get it. Then he comes and takes it back again. Back and forth! I'm victorious one minute, and defeated the next. *Enough of this taffy pull with the enemy!*

You and I must be of the mindset that when God delivers us, we must arm ourselves to maintain our deliverance. We must have scriptures ready to apply to our situation.

When God delivers us from depression, we must not wait until the enemy tries to bring depression back. We must arm ourselves with **Isaiah 26:3**, *"Thou wilt keep him in perfect peace, whose mind is stayed on thee: because he trusteth in thee!"* When God delivers us from a bad relationship, we are not going to wait until he or she comes knocking at our door, but we are going to have a scripture waiting. When God delivers us from drinking or smoking, we are not going to wait until the urge comes back. We are going to march straight to that refrigerator, and get that liquor and pour it out! We are going to throw those cigarettes away! We are going to be proactive; participating in maintaining our victory!

Chapter 11

How to Avoid Non-Productive Cycles

How to Avoid Non-Productive Cycles

And the Lord spake unto me saying, "Ye have compassed this mountain long enough, turn you northward!"
(Deuteronomy 2:2-3)

Have you ever been stuck? We have all had areas in our lives that were not moving; not going forward. Sometimes those areas develop into what I call non-productive cycles in our lives.

Defined, a non-productive cycle is a situation that is recurring with no improvement. Typically, non-productive cycles have three characteristics:

1. They keep reoccurring.
2. They are very lengthy.
3. There is no improvement.

We can become involved in non-productive cycles in many areas of our lives. For example, in our parenting. Our adult children get in trouble and we bail them out. They get in trouble again, and we bail them out again. They get in trouble over and over again and we constantly rescue them. That is a non-productive cycle.

Finances are also areas that can become non-productive cycles. We get out of debt. We pay the credit cards off. Then we charge them all up again. That is a non-productive cycle.

We can become involved in non-productive cycles even in our Christian tests and trials. When we fail the same test over and over again or when we never quite make it through that trial, that is a non-productive cycle. It just cycles around and around and around again.

There is only one way to break non-productive cycles in our lives; we must respond to the situation differently. Sometimes we must let that child experience the consequences of his or her actions and refuse to bail them out over and over again. We may have to pay off the credit cards and then cut them up. We must determine that we are going to pass that trial or that test. This time we're going to get beyond it and get to that next level that God has for us. However, we cannot get there by responding the same way as we have in the past. We must respond differently and in a manner that promotes positive change.

Remember the story of David and Goliath? **I Samuel 17** describes a time that the Philistines and the Israelites were at war. The Philistines were on one side and the Israelites were on the other side. Between them was a valley or a trench. Three of Jessie's sons were also involved in the war.

However, no serious fighting had taken place. The Bible describes them as standing on their respective sides and exchanging insults. Apparently, no one took this war very seriously. In fact, Jessie sent young David with a picnic lunch for his brothers.

To substantiate the fact that there was no warfare occurring, young David was allowed to go directly where the men were supposed to be engaged in war and allowed to converse with his brothers and the other soldiers.

The first thing that David did was to assess the war. David identified a non-productive cycle, because here they were 40 days into the war and there was no decisive victory.

David did something differently! He used a different strategy and a different weapon. With a mere slingshot and a few smooth stones, he killed the giant and broke the cycle.

You and I must identify every non-productive cycle in our lives, because the bad news is that the enemy takes non-productive cycles and turns them into strongholds.

As you are reading this, you have probably already identified some non-productive cycles in your life. Break those cycles one by one! Remember, it only takes *one time* of responding differently to break a non-productive cycle. Break that cycle and kill that giant!

Chapter 12

Spiritual Warfare

Spiritual Warfare

For though we walk in the flesh, we do not war after the flesh: For the weapons of our warfare are not carnal, but mighty through God to the pulling down of strongholds: Casting down imaginations, and every high thing that exalteth itself against the knowledge of God, and bringing into captivity every thought to the obedience of Christ.
(II Corinthians 10:3-5)

Spiritual warfare is the ongoing battle between believers and Satan and his host of demons.[6] Satan's kingdom is a highly systematized empire of evil composed of high ranking evil spirits with supernatural power. Satan and his demons attempt to bring dishonor to God's name in the earth and destruction and deception to all those who love and serve Him.

Satan is described as the god of this world. He is depicted as the prince of the power of the air, which is the dwelling place and medium of his evil influences. Since Satan is the prince of the power of the air, these wicked spirits in high places are often understood to be the collective organization of all of Satan's evil spirits working evil and mischief and operating in the very atmosphere in which we live. However, his power is limited, always under the sovereign control of God, and is temporary.

The Believer's Call to Spiritual Warfare

We as believers are involved in a spiritual warfare that can only be waged by the power of the Holy Spirit. The baptism in the Holy Spirit is God's provision for releasing the power of the Holy Spirit into the believer's life. This "dunamis power" designates power in action.

In **Romans 6:16**, Paul emphasizes the necessity for continual warfare against anything or anyone who would limit the work of God in our lives. *"Know ye not, that to whom ye yield yourselves servants to obey, his servants, ye are to whom ye obey; whether of sin unto death, or of obedience unto righteousness?"*

Paul sees the believer's life as an intense struggle that requires persevering in contending with adversaries of the gospel. We are called to defend the gospel in whatever occupation God has placed us—never compromising the original truth of the gospel.

The believer's warfare must be fought against:

1) Satan and his forces
2) The flesh
3) Worldly temptations

Allegiance to Christ demands a constant readiness to expose, resist, and speak against wickedness in all forms.

What are the Weapons of our Warfare?

Spiritual warfare is not about a technique to defeat Satan and his demons, but, being able to "*stand*" against the wiles of the devil by the power of the Holy Spirit. Through the power of the Holy Spirit we can overcome evil, sin, Satan, trials, temptations, sorrow, persecution, and false teachings. Believers have no reason to live in fear of Satan or evil spirits. He can hinder, but he cannot defeat us as long as we "*utilize*" the spiritual weapons God has provided for us.

The only weapons adequate to destroy the fortresses of Satan are those which God gives in **Ephesians 6:14-18:** *"Stand therefore, having your loins girt about with truth, and having on the breastplate of righteousness; And your feet shod with the preparation of the gospel of peace; Above all, taking the shield of faith, wherewith ye shall be able to quench all the fiery darts of the wicked. And take the helmet of salvation, and the sword of the Spirit, which is the word of God: Praying always with all prayer and supplication in the Spirit."*

These weapons are powerful because they are God-given:

Truth

The revealed Word of God; The Gospel of Jesus Christ.

The Breast Plate of Righteousness

Covered and protected by the principles of true holiness, the precepts of God, and conformity to the will of God.

The Preparation of the Gospel of Peace

Preparation indicates readiness to do God's will and proclaim the Gospel of Peace. It is called the "Gospel of Peace" because it establishes peace between God and man and announces peace and goodwill to the universe. It comes with authority, reveals God's righteousness, and creates faith.

The Shield of Faith

Faith is our God given spiritual resource for warfare. It gives us complete confidence that Satan's power can be broken in any specific area of his domain. It puts God between us and the enemy (as does a shield). This faith in action counters, diminishes, and destroys every evil weapon or influence the devil projects our way.

The Helmet of Salvation

The "Helmet of Salvation" is expressed as the "Hope of Salvation." The assurance of conquering every adversary and of overcoming every difficulty, through the blood of the Lamb. It is as a helmet that protects the head which cannot be penetrated. The blows of the battle-axe cannot split it, divide, or separate it. We have this "hope" of eternal life because we believe on Jesus, the Son of God.

The Sword of the Spirit

The "Sword of the Spirit," which is the "Word of God," is our offensive weapon provided by the Holy Spirit. It is the revelation which God has given of Himself. The ability to use this sword in times of temptation and adversities cuts in pieces the snares of the adversary.

Prayer

When we pray, we keep the lines of communication open with God. Persistent prayer is necessary to successfully resist principalities, powers, rulers of darkness in the world, and spiritual wickedness in high places. We must pray in public, in private, with our families, constantly in our hearts, and also audibly, strongly appealing to God until the evil is gone or the good communicated.

The purpose of this collection of defensive covering is for us to hold our ground firmly, completely, gloriously, and victoriously. Always ready to repel any attack from Satan and his forces. Putting on the whole armor prepares us for each day of victory. Putting on the whole armor of God is the believer's assurance of successful warfare against Satan and his forces of evil!

Chapter 13

Destiny and Purpose

Destiny and Purpose

And when Joseph's brethren saw that their father was dead, they said, Joseph will peradventure hate us, and will certainly requite us all the evil which we did unto him. And they sent a messenger unto Joseph, saying, Thy father did command before he died, saying, So shall ye say unto Joseph, Forgive, I pray thee now, the trespass of thy brethren, and their sin; for they did unto thee evil: and now, we pray thee, forgive the trespass of the servants of the God of thy father. And Joseph wept when they spake unto him.

And his brethren also went and fell down before his face; and they said, Behold, we be thy servants. And Joseph said unto them, Fear not: for am I in the place of God? But as for you, ye thought evil against me; but God meant it unto good, to bring to pass, as it is this day, to save much people alive.
(Genesis 50:15-20)

We are all familiar with the story of Joseph. How at the age of 17, God begins to reveal himself to this young man. God deals with Joseph in a series of dreams, and in each of the dreams, Joseph seems to have preeminence over his brothers and even his parents. In fact, he is *always* the star of the dreams. The brothers become consumed with jealousy and envy and become haters. They devise a plan and a plot to do away with Joseph.

To expedite this story, Joseph is thrown into a pit by his brothers. From the pit, he is sold into slavery. From slavery, he advances to Potiphar's house where he is approached and falsely accused by Potiphar's wife, and then thrown into prison. All the while, God's plan is unfolding and His purpose for Joseph's life and Joseph's destiny is being shaped and developed.

Joseph, after interpreting Pharaoh's dream, is released from prison and he rises to power. God positions him as ruler over the vast wealth of Pharaoh and Joseph becomes a man of authority and prestige.

Joseph implements a strategy that saves an entire region from starvation, including his estranged family. Joseph's brother come before him expecting the worst; expecting him to retaliate; expecting him to exact revenge.

However, somewhere in the midst of the struggles that Joseph faced in his life since being separated from his family, somewhere in the process of having been thrown in the pit, somewhere in the midst of being sold into slavery, somewhere in the midst of being falsely accused, and even during his prison sentence, Joseph realizes and he comes to understand that that there is a higher purpose for his life. There is a higher goal. *God had destiny and purpose for his life!*

Who would have believed that the events in Joseph's life, (both negative and positive) would somehow, someway bring Joseph from the pit all the way to the palace? From the day that God formed Joseph in his mother's womb, He had a well crafted plan for Joseph's life.

That is why we cannot isolate any one incident in our lives and embrace it as our fate. The Bible says that all things work together for the good of those who love the Lord and who are the called according to His purpose. Maybe in isolation, some of the things that we encounter look pretty devastating, but collectively, they work for our good.

No matter what we may be facing right now, in the grand scheme of things, the plan that God has for our lives is far greater than what we are going through, no matter how disconnected it appears, no matter how out of sync it may be, no matter how off the wall. All we really need to know is that God is in perfect control and He is going to bring us to that expected end. *We must trust God!*

What you and I must realize is that God is not limited, nor is He restricted by the same constraints as we. In fact, He does not have to work in chronological order. He does not have to work sequentially. And He is not date and time oriented by a calendar or by a watch. Sometimes the cart does come *before* the horse where is God is concerned.

Our destiny and our purpose are not predicated on the tangible things that we can see, hear and feel. There is another realm where there is an enormous amount of activity occurring! God is in the process of doing great things for us. He has arranged some divine connections for our lives. It's not by might, nor by power, it is by my spirit saith the Lord!

I often wonder how I escaped all of the traps and snares that the enemy laid out for me early in my life. A skinny, black barefooted little girl living in extreme poverty in public housing. Surrounded by drugs, gangs, guns, poverty, and violence. I could have been the Poster Child for defeat. But God!

Why do you think that God sustained you through everything you've been through? It is because He has an expected end for you. He knew you couldn't do it from a hospital bed, so He raised you up! He knew you couldn't do it from the end of a bottle or from the end of a needle, so he delivered you! All of us have had close calls where even the enemy is looking at us scratching his head, wondering how in the world did they come out of *that*.

There is only one thing that will prevent us from fulfilling our destiny: If *WE* give up!

Chapter 14

FAITH

Faith

Blessed be the God and Father of our Lord Jesus Christ, which according to His abundant mercy hath begotten us again unto a lively hope by the resurrection of Jesus Christ from the dead, to an inheritance incorruptible, and undefiled, and that fadeth not away, reserved in heaven for you. Who are kept by the power of God through faith unto salvation ready to be revealed in the last time. Wherein ye greatly rejoice, though now for a season, if need be, ye are in heaviness through manifold temptations. That the trial of your faith, being much more precious than of gold that perisheth, though it be tried with fire, might be found unto praise and honor and glory at the appearing of Jesus Christ.
(I Peter 1:3-7)

Faith is defined as complete confidence, reliance, or trust in someone or something. Faith is paramount because Faith is where it all began for us as believers. It is the beginning of it all because our first step towards God was a step in faith.

The Bible declares that without faith it is impossible to please God, for he that cometh to God must *believe* first of all, that He (God) *IS* and that He is a rewarder of them that diligently seek Him.

In the opening passage of scripture, the Christians were being persecuted by the Roman Government. When Nero came into power, he began to persecute them as well. Nero was a heartless, ruthless ruler.

He gave strict orders to have the Christians hunted down. After they were captured, some were tortured and others were killed. In an attempt to escape this mad man, the Christians began scattering all over Europe.

What was Nero's goal? Though he tortured some of them, he was not really interested in their suffering. Though he killed some of them, he was not really after their lives. He was after their faith in God! That is why Peter referred to what they were experiencing at the hands of Nero as a trial of their faith.

Many of us have experienced trials of our very faith. I am not talking about when we are being tried in maybe one aspect of our faith, and then we recover. I am talking about when our *entire* belief system is under fire! When our confidence in God is being shaken to the core! When the enemy goes for the jugular vein of our Christian walk which is our faith in God! It is those times that are the defining moments that determine whether we will stay with God or whether we are going to walk away from Him.

When the enemy was allowed to attack Job, he wasn't after Job's children, although they were destroyed. He wasn't after

Job's marriage, although it became completely dysfunctional. He wasn't even after Job's health, although it was extremely compromised. The enemy was after Job's faith. He was after Job's confidence in God. That is why he asked God to remove the hedge from around Job. In other words, his plan was to destroy Job's faith base.

Let us revisit the Christians who were mentioned in **I Peter**. History records that although the persecution initiated by Nero was designed to diminish their faith, the persecution actually caused an increase in their commitment and devotion to God.

Why? Because they had a history with God! And our history with God tells us that anything that comes our way must first be sifted through the hand of God! And although our faith is tried by fire, when the fire dies down, *And it will*! When the smoke clears, *And it will!* When the fiery trial ends, *And it will*; We will emerge from the fire as pure gold, with our faith intact. We might not have the testimony of the 3 Hebrew boys! We may very well smell like smoke! Our hair may very well be singed! We may look as though we've been in a fire! But *out* is *out!*

We must summon strength from deep down inside of us and be encouraged by what we know about our God.

Many times, suffering occurs to prove or authenticate our faith. God does not give us a pseudo faith. God takes our reality (whatever that reality is) and changes it into a different reality!

You know what the Lord hopes to find when He comes back? He is not looking for our earthly accomplishments, although those accomplishments may be wonderful. But Jesus asks this question of us: *"When the Son of Man cometh, shall He find faith on the earth?"*

Chapter 15

Unity Within the Body of Christ

Unity Within the Body of Christ

Behold how good and how pleasant it is for brethren to dwell together in unity.
(Psalm 133:1)

Unity is paramount in the body of Christ. It is so vitally important that it is the first issue that Paul addresses in the 1st book of Corinthians and he goes on to devote 4 entire chapters to the subject.

Paul wrote in **1 Corinthians 1:10**, *"But I urge and entreat you, brethren, by the name of our Lord Jesus Christ, that all of you be in perfect harmony, and full agreement in what you say, and that there be no dissensions, or factions, or divisions among you, but that you be perfectly united in your common understanding and in your opinions and judgments."*

Paul was not saying that we will all have the same, exact thoughts or personalities, because we are all different and unique; But what Paul was saying is that we must strive to be on one accord and united in purpose.

What occurred in the Corinthian church is a case and point of what divisiveness can do to the body of Christ. The enemy is not all that innovative! The Bible says that we are not ignorant concerning his devices. He may use a different strategy, but he uses the same tools or devices and division is a weapon and a device that the enemy uses on the body of Christ consistently.

Division is one of the *major* barriers to unity that the enemy uses. The Corinthian church got caught up in personalities. Some wanted Paul, some wanted Apollos, and some wanted Peter. Let's face it; we all may have our preferences in terms of whose delivery we prefer. There may be a certain style of preaching or a certain style of teaching that we prefer, but the word of God is the word of God. No one has a monopoly on the word and the word did not originate with any of us. We must realize that whoever is delivering the word is merely a vessel being used of God.

Romans 16:17 makes a very strong statement. That passage admonishes us to mark them which cause division among us and avoid them.

Division is a tactic of the worldly system. Almost everything that the world does is based on the inclusion of a certain group and the exclusion of another group.

It reminds me of when we were children and whenever there was a game, the captains of the teams had to choose up sides. It can be a very cruel method and it is devastating to a child. When I was younger, I was very small and not very athletic, so when the time came to choose, I was one of the last ones chosen — if I was chosen at all. I remember feeling left out and not quite good enough. I often went home crushed and devastated thinking, "What is wrong with me?"

If we are not careful, the enemy would have us use those same tactics in the church where we form cliques, groups, and factions. Beloved, it ought not to be! No one is dispensable where God is concerned! We are all (every one of us) valuable to Him!

There was also competition concerning gifts in the Corinthian Church. **1 Corinthians 12:4** in the Amplified reminds us that, *"There are distinctive varieties and distributions of endowments (gifts, extraordinary powers distinguishing certain Christians, due to the power of divine grace operating in their souls by the Holy Spirit) and they vary, but the Holy Spirit remains the same. And there are distinctive varieties of service and ministration, but it is the same Lord Who is served. And there are distinctive varieties of operation of working to accomplish things, but it is the same God Who inspires and energizes them all in all. But to each one is given the manifestation of the Holy Spirit the evidence, the spiritual illumination of the Spirit for good and profit."*

Later in that passage, Paul goes on to explain that we are *"Collectively Christ's body and individually we are members of it, each part severally and distinct; each with his own place and function."* Which means that we are not enemies and in competition with one another, but we are allies.

Those of you who are in the medical field know that certain conditions of the body are caused by a deficient immune system. When the body begins to fight against itself, that is when diseases occur. Paul describes our physical bodies as a sort of metaphor of the church. Just as the physical body is dysfunctional when one of its members is not functioning properly, so it is in the church. Every member of the body serves a unique and specific function. But then here is the key; it must operate in conjunction with the other members. Because the body of Christ is the catalyst through which God works.

Finally, the Corinthian church had turf issues. When we are given an assignment, title or position, we can become quite territorial, can't we? This is *my* area, this is *my* choir, this is *my* kitchen. We are aware that there must be clear distinct lines of responsibilities. But sometimes there may be an overlapping of assignments. Some elements of my assignment might spill over into yours.

For example, if I am in charge of the coffee and you are in charge of the donuts and both the coffee and the donuts are served in the kitchen, sometime or another, we are BOTH going to be in the kitchen!

Paul admonishes us to *endeavor* to keep the unity of the spirit, because there are certain elements of unity that are not going to be automatic. The word “endeavor” means to exert effort. Paul is telling us to exert effort so that we can both build and maintain unity. Let us all identify ways in which to promote and to implement unity. Above all, let us support one another unconditionally in love, because love supplies the cohesion that makes unity possible.

Chapter 16

Corporate Worship

Corporate Worship

And He came to Nazareth, where He had been brought up, and as His custom was, He went into the synagogue on the Sabbath day, and stood up for to read.
(St. Luke 4:16)

Just how important is corporate worship? Well, Jesus went to church. **St. Matthew 12:9** states, *"And when He was departed thence, He went into their synagogue."* **St. Mark 1:21** states, *"And they went into Capernaum, and straightway on the Sabbath day, He entered into the synagogue, and taught."* **St. Luke 4:16** states, *"And He came to Nazareth, where He had been brought up, and as His custom was, He went into the synagogue on the Sabbath day, and stood up for to read."*

If Jesus found it crucial to attend church, what about us? In **Hebrews 10:25**, the Bible says that we should not forsake the assembling of ourselves together. Not only that, but we are also admonished to accelerate our participation in corporate worship as we see the end times approaching.

What we are observing is somewhat of a paradox. These are, indeed, the end times. However, the attendance in our local churches is decreasing. It is disheartening that most churches have an active roll and an inactive roll. There may be 100 members, but only 50 people may attend church on a regular basis.

When attendance drops that drastically, the Pastor does the only thing he can do, and that is to decrease the amount of services. He soon tires of trying to conduct a church service with just his wife and children in attendance. He can no longer continue to accrue the expense of utilities in an empty church. Therefore, Pastors who typically held service 2 or 3 times a week, have decreased it to once a week, and that is usually on Sunday.

Many times, Pastors are competing with all of the Tele-Evangelists on television. In the wake of all of the church programs on television, more and more people are staying home and their excuse is, "Why go to church when I can watch it on television?"

Let me hasten to add that there is absolutely nothing wrong with watching the church programs that come on television. They are hosted by some of the most gifted and anointed ministers. However, those programs were only designed to supplement and enhance. They were never designed to replace corporate worship. There is nothing quite like being in the presence of God and worshipping Him in the presence of other believers.

Is there any benefit in watching Tele-Evangelists? Absolutely! However, there is an exponential power and anointing that we will only experience when we worship as a corporate body that we will not experience any other way.

There are a lot of excuses as to why people do not attend church on a regular basis. All of these excuses can be easily dispelled:

Excuse #1: I don't go to Church because I've been hurt.

Let me ask a question. What did God do to you that you no longer want to visit His house?

Excuse #2: I just can't seem to find the right church.

You are looking for a perfect church. And excuse my vernacular, but "There ain't no such animal!" Every church has its own set of issues and issues are not unique to any specific church.

Excuse #3: Nobody cares whether I come to church or not.

You could not be more mistaken! God knows and He cares and He misses you when you are not there. Many times, God may have given a sister or a brother a word for you specific to your situation. Or He has sent a sister or a brother to touch and agree with you in prayer concerning an issue in which you have been struggling. You may need to hear a testimony or someone will sing a song that will lift your spirits. The Pastor may preach just the exact word that reveals the answer you need to your situation.

After Solomon completed the building of the temple, The Lord said in I Kings 9:3, *"I have hallowed this house, to put my name there forever, and mine eyes and my heart shall be there perpetually."*

I challenge anyone who is reading this book to attend church this week. If you are not ill or otherwise incapacitated, go to church this week. If you left your former church with unresolved issues, go to that Pastor and communicate with him! If he is a Pastor after God's own heart, he will listen.

If you have fallen into error while you were away, you may feel a little uncomfortable and it may be a little awkward at first, but ask the Lord for forgiveness. In fact, do it right now! Then get everything prepared the night before Worship Service. You don't want to be late!

"I was glad when they said unto me, Let us go into the house of the Lord!" Psalm 122:1

Chapter 17

The Promise
The Purpose and The Power of The Holy Spirit

The Promise, The Purpose, and The Power of The Holy Spirit

But ye shall receive power, after that the Holy Ghost is come upon you: and ye shall be witnesses unto Me both in Jerusalem, and in all Judaea, and in Samaria, and unto the uttermost part of the earth.
(Acts 1:8)

God's desire is for us to be victorious in our walk with Him. Therefore, He has many means through which He both empowers and equips us for service: through His word, through fasting, through prayer, through fellowship with believers, and through His spirit.

The Bible refers to the Spirit of God as the Holy Ghost or the Holy Spirit. These two terms are used interchangeably in scripture. Jesus also called Him the Comforter.

The Holy Spirit is not a trend or a fad. The Holy Spirit is not someone who is "In Vogue" today and out the next day, but He plays a very significant role in our walk with the Lord and He is vital to our success as believers. Quite frankly without Him, we could not remain saved for very long.

We cannot stop at repentance. Repenting and receiving the Holy Spirit are two separate and distinct acts. However, it is the *same* spirit that does the work. The Holy Spirit does the drawing, convicts us of our sins, and sanctifies or purifies us.

There may be instances *before* we are completely filled, when the Holy Spirit may overshadow us and we may feel His presence. But being filled with the Holy Spirit is *subsequent* to or comes *after* conversion.

Before we explore the *Promise*, the *Purpose*, and the *Power* of the Holy Spirit, let us delineate other aspects of the Holy Spirit:[7]

- Who is the Holy Spirit?
- Was the gift of the Holy Spirit for the disciples only?
- What are the conditions for receiving the Holy Spirit?
- How does one receive the Holy Spirit?
- What is the *sign* of the Holy Spirit and what is the *evidence* of the Holy Spirit?

Who is the Holy Spirit?

The Holy Spirit is the third Person of the Trinity.

1 John 5:7

"For there are three that bear record in heaven; the Father [God], the Word [Jesus], and the Holy Ghost: and these three are one."

The scripture that best identifies these three entities is **St. Luke 3:22**: *"And the Holy Ghost descended in a bodily shape like a dove upon Him, and a voice came from heaven, which said, Thou art My beloved Son; in thee I am well pleased."*

He was present during creation.

Genesis 1:2

"And the earth was without form, and void; and darkness was upon the face of the deep. And the Spirit of God moved upon the face of the waters."

He is involved in the redemption of man.

St. John 3:5

"Verily, verily, I say unto thee, except a man be born of water and of the Spirit, he cannot enter into the kingdom of God."

Was the gift of the Holy Spirit for the Disciples only?

No. After the disciples were filled with the Holy Spirit, those who observed them were astonished because they heard the disciples speak in their language. Some even accused the disciples of being drunk. Peter immediately stood up and preached his very first sermon. Peter was so convincing, that the people were convicted of their sins. They asked Peter, *"What must we do?"* Peter instructed them in **Acts 2:38**, to *"Repent, and be baptized every one of you in the name of Jesus Christ for the remission of sins, and ye shall receive the gift of the Holy Ghost."*

After giving them these instructions, Peter assured them in **Acts 2:39**, *"For the Promise is unto you, and to your children, and to all that are afar off, even as many as the Lord our God shall call."*

What are the conditions for receiving the Holy Spirit?

The only condition for receiving the Holy Spirit is *we must be saved!* Everyone who received the Holy Spirit in the scriptures was saved. That is the *only* condition. Water baptism *is not* a precursor or condition for being filled with the Holy Spirit.

When the Holy Spirit fell in the midst of Peter's sermon to the Gentiles in **Acts 10:47-48**, Peter asked those disciples who were with him, *"Can any man forbid water, that these should not be baptized, who have received the Holy Ghost as well as we? And he commanded them to be baptized in the name of the Lord."* These gentiles *had not* been baptized in water yet.

Just to clarify: The above passage substantiates two important facts:

1. We can be filled with the Holy Spirit *before* we have been baptized in water.
2. When Peter emphasized being baptized in the name of Jesus Christ for the remission of sins, he was not giving a *formula* for baptism.

But because these people were baptized unto John's baptism, they then had to be baptized unto Jesus' baptism. Why? Because it was an outward act, expression, and symbol of Jesus dying and being raised from the dead. It indicated that they both believed on and accepted Jesus as their savior for the remission of their sins, and that they were burying the old man and rising up a new man.

How does one receive the Holy Spirit?

By asking for Him
St. Luke 11:9-13

"And I say unto you ask, and it shall be given you, seek and ye shall find, knock and it shall be opened unto you. For every one that asketh receiveth, and he that seeketh findeth, and to him that kocketh it shall be opened. If a son shall ask bread of any of you that is a Father, will he give him a stone? Or if he ask a fish, will he for a fish give him a serpent? Or if he shall ask an egg, will he offer him a scorpion? If ye then being evil, know how to give good gifts unto your children, how much more shall your heavenly Father give the Holy Spirit to them that ask him?"

By the laying on of hands
Acts 8:14-17

"Now when the apostles which were at Jerusalem heard that Samaria had received the word of God, they sent unto them Peter and John. Who when they were come down, prayed for them, that they might receive the Holy Ghost. For as yet He was fallen upon none of them, only they were baptized in the name of the Lord Jesus. Then laid they their hands on them, and they received the Holy Ghost."

Through hearing the preached word of God
Acts 10:43-46

"To him give all the prophets witness, that through His name, whosoever believeth in Him shall receive remission of sins. While Peter YET spake these words, the Holy Ghost fell on all them which heard the word. And they of the circumcision which believed were astonished, as many as came with Peter, because that on the Gentiles also was poured out the gift of the Holy Ghost. For they heard them speak with tongues and magnify God."

Other places/Other ways

While in the shower, in the bed, at work, at school, at the bus-stop, in the car (pull over first, please!)

And through a process known as "tarrying" which is how I received Him. The word *tarry* simply means to wait. We know that the Holy Spirit is already here, so what was this tarrying process? The old saints back in the day felt that in order to be in a receptive spirit, we must rid ourselves of all distractions. This included "waiting" before the Lord at the altar. They would stand with us and encourage us to believe, focus on God, and invoke His presence. Guess what? It works and *many* of us received Him that way!

What is the *sign* of the Holy Spirit and what is the *evidence* of the Holy Spirit?

Let us define *sign* and *evidence*, as they are often used interchangeably, but there is a slight difference:

Sign: A visible indication that something has occurred.

Evidence: To demonstrate by one's behavior, attitude, or external attributes. To further clarify, *speaking in other tongues* is a sign or an indication that someone has experienced the gift of the Holy Spirit. However, evidence is the manner in which the Holy Spirit manifests Himself in the life of the believer *if* allowed.

How does He do this? What should we expect to observe in one who has received the Holy Spirit? The evidence of having the indwelling of the Holy Spirit is the Fruit of the Spirit manifested in our behavior, attitude, and external attributes.

In **Galatians 5:22-23**, the apostle Paul lists 9 components of the Fruit of the Spirit:

- Love: Active good will, expressed toward God and man
- Joy: Gladness, delight, especially in response to God
- Peace: Tranquility, harmony, with God and our fellow man
- Longsuffering: Patience, forbearance, self-restraint
- Gentleness: Sweetness of temper towards others
- Goodness: Generosity that reaches beyond giving what is one's due
- Faith: The virtue of reliability
- Meekness: A humble and kind demeanor
- Temperance: Self-control of one's desires and appetites

Also in **Romans 14:17** and **15:13**, Paul mentions others, such as righteousness and hope. In **2 Peter 1:5-8**, Peter mentions faith, virtue, knowledge, temperance, patience, Godliness, brotherly kindness, and charity (love).

You will find that people who are considered *moral* may display some of these attributes. However, believers who are full of the Holy Spirit display them all; perhaps in varying degrees; but believers who are full of the Holy Spirit display them *all*!

The Promise

The first mention of the promise of the Holy Spirit in the New Testament can be found in **St. Matthew 3:11.** John said, *"I indeed baptize you with water, but He that cometh after me is mightier than I, whose shoes I am not worthy to bear: He shall baptize you with the Holy Ghost and with fire."*

One of the last commissions of Jesus to His disciples just before He went away to be with the Father can be found in **St. Luke 24:49**, He told His disciples, *"And, behold, I send the promise of my Father upon you: but tarry ye in the city of Jerusalem, until ye be endued with power from on high."*

In **St. John 14:16-18a**, Jesus told His disciples, *"And I will pray the Father, and He shall give you another Comforter, that he may abide with you forever; Even the Spirit of truth; whom the world cannot receive, because It seeth him not, neither knoweth* *him; but ye know him; for he dwelleth with you, and shall be in you. I will not leave you comfortless."*

And in **St. John 16:7b,** Jesus also told His disciples, *"It is expedient for you that I go away, for if I go not away the Comforter will not come unto you, but if I depart, I will send him unto you."*

Finally, before Jesus ascended, in **St. John 20:22**, it is recorded, *"And when He had said this, He breathed on them, and saith unto them, 'Receive ye the Holy Ghost.'"*

The Purpose

The Holy Spirit has many functions in the life of the believer:

As a teacher
St. John 14:26

"But the Comforter, which is the Holy Ghost, whom the Father will send in my name, he shall teach you all things, and bring all things to your remembrance, whatsoever I have said unto you."

As a guide
St. John 16:13

"Howbeit when he, the Spirit of truth, is come, he will guide you into all truth: for he shall not speak of himself; but whatsoever he shall hear, that shall he speak: and he will shew you things to come."

As an intercessor
Romans 8:26

"Likewise the Spirit also helpeth our infirmities: for we know not what we should pray for as we ought: but the Spirit itself maketh intercession for us with groanings which cannot be uttered."

The Power

Acts 1:8

"But ye shall receive power, after that the Holy Ghost is come upon you: and ye shall be witnesses unto me both in Jerusalem, and in all Judaea, and in Samaria, and unto the uttermost part of the earth."

The Holy Spirit absolutely empowers us and we are strengthened by Him. **Romans 8:13**, lets us know that through Him, we are able to put to death the deeds of the body.

My Pastor made an analogy contrasting the absence of the Holy Spirit in our lives to the missing ingredients of a cake. When we are baking a cake and we forget to include an important ingredient, the cake is going to be incomplete. If we omit the baking powder, the cake will not rise. If we omit the sugar, the cake will not be sweet. If we omit the eggs, we will have a very dense cake.

We cannot be very effective or powerful in the absence of God's Spirit dwelling on the inside of us and operating freely in our lives.

Chapter 18

PRAYER

Prayer

And He spake a parable unto them to this end that men ought always to pray...
(St. Luke 18:1)

Prayer defined is simply dialogue between God and man. Though prayer is simple in its definition, it is extremely powerful in its execution. The Bible says that prayer is dynamic and effective!

James 5:16b

"The earnest heartfelt, continued prayer of a righteous man makes tremendous power available dynamic in its working."

James 5:17

"Elijah was a human being with a nature such as we have, with feelings, affections, and a constitution like ours; and he prayed earnestly for it not to rain, and no rain fell on the earth for three years and six months."

James 5:18

"And then he prayed again and the heavens supplied rain and the land produced its crops as usual."

What should we pray for?

Everything! All issues, problems, situations, and circumstances. **Philippians 4:6** tells us *"Do not fret or have any* *anxiety about anything, but in every circumstance and in everything, by prayer and petition, definite requests, with thanksgiving, continue to make your wants known to God."*

What should we say?

In **St. Matthew 6:7-9**, the Bible tells us, *"And when you pray, do not heap up phrases multiply words, repeating the same ones over and over as the Gentiles do, for they think they will be heard for their much speaking. Do not be like them, for your Father knows what you need before you ask Him. Pray therefore like this."* (Jesus proceeds to teach them a prayer model).

What posture should we use?

It does not matter! We can bow, bend, sit, stand, kneel, or lay prostrate before the Lord.

How long should we pray?

It does not matter! The main thing is to communicate with God. That includes talking to Him and then being quiet and allowing Him to talk to us.

Conditions to Prayer

We must pray in God's will
1 John 5:14-15

"And this is the confidence the assurance, the privilege of boldness which we have in Him; we are sure that if we ask anything make any request according to His will in agreement with

His own plan, He listens to and hears us. And if we know that He listens to us in whatever we ask, we also know that we have the requests made of Him."

We must be persistent
St. Luke 18:1-8a

Also Jesus told them a parable to the effect that they ought always to pray and not to turn coward, faint, lose heart, and give up. He said, "In a certain city there was a judge who neither reverenced and feared God nor respected or considered man. And there was a widow in that city who kept coming to him and saying, 'Protect and defend and give me justice against my adversary.'

"And for a time he would not; but later he said to himself, 'Though I have neither reverence or fear for God nor respect or consideration for man, yet because this widow continues to bother me, I will defend and protect and avenge her, lest she give me intolerable annoyance and wear me out by her continual coming or at the last she come and rail on me or assault me or strangle me.'" Then the Lord said, "Listen to what the unjust judge says!"

"And will not our just God defend and protect and avenge His elect His chosen ones, who cry to Him day and night? Will He defer them and delay help on their behalf? I tell you, He will defend and protect and avenge them speedily."

Obstacles to Prayer

Disobedience
Psalm 66:18

"If I regard iniquity in my heart, the Lord will not hear me."

Isaiah 1:15

"And when you spread forth your hands in prayer, imploring help, I will hide My eyes from you; even though you make many prayers, I will not hear."

Lack of Faith
James 1:5-6

"If any of you is deficient in wisdom, let him ask of the giving God who gives to everyone liberally and ungrudgingly, without reproaching or faultfinding, and it will be given him."

"Only it must be in faith that he asks with no wavering no hesitating, no doubting. For the one who wavers hesitates, doubts is like the billowing surge out at sea that is blown hither and thither and tossed by the wind."

Failure to Ask
James 4:2b

"You do not have, because you do not ask."

Wrong Motive
James 4:3

"You do ask, and yet fail to receive, because you ask with wrong purpose and evil, selfish motives. Your intention is when

you get what you desire to spend it in sensual pleasures."

St. Matthew 6:5-6

"Also when you pray, you must not be like the hypocrites, for they love to pray standing in the synagogues, and on the corners of the streets, that they may be seen by people. Truly I tell you, they have their reward in full already. But when you pray, go into your most private room, and closing the door, pray to your Father, Who is in secret; and your Father, Who sees in secret, will reward you in the open."

Unforgiveness
St. Matthew 5:23-24

"So if when you are offering your gift at the altar you there remember that your brother has any grievance against you, Leave your gift at the altar and go. First make peace with your brother, and then come back and present your gift."

St. Matthew 6:14-15

"For if you forgive people their trespasses their reckless and willful sins leaving them, letting them go, and giving up resentment, your heavenly Father will also forgive you. But if you do not forgive others their trespasses their reckless and willful sins, leaving them, letting them go, and giving up resentment, neither will your Father forgive you your trespasses."

Different Types of Prayer

The Prayer Of Supplication

The Prayer of Supplication is rendered when we petition God for spiritual or natural provision, either for ourselves or on the behalf of someone else.

The Prayer Of Intercession

The Prayer of Intercession is a prayer of mediation. We are actually standing in proxy for someone else and petitioning God on their behalf.

The Prayer Of Faith

The Prayer of Faith is a prayer that exercises and demonstrates our trust and confidence in God for a particular situation. This prayer is based totally on His word.

The Prayer Of Agreement

The Prayer of Agreement is rendered by two or more people who pray in unity, with one accord, and with one purpose about a specific condition, problem, or situation. The primary plea in this prayer is for God's will to be done.

The Prayer Of Praise And Thanksgiving

In this prayer, we ask nothing for ourselves. We focus completely on God. We recognize who He is and what He has done in our lives. Then we praise Him for who He is and for what He has done in our lives. And finally, we thank Him for who He is and for what He has done in our lives. [8]

Chapter 19

FASTING

Fasting

Is not this the fast that I have chosen? To loose the bands of wickedness, to undo the heavy burdens, and to let the oppressed go free, and that ye break every yoke?
(Isaiah 58:6)

Fasting is powerful! Yokes can be broken and lives transformed through fasting. I am convinced that when God's people fast, God will hear from heaven and intervene on our behalf in our lives, our churches, our communities, and even in our world. And yet fasting is one of the most neglected spiritual essentials and seemingly no longer has the same impact that it once had.

One of the reasons is that we have made fasting so complicated and we have so many variations of it: The Daniel fast, the juice fast, the water fast, the complete fast, the partial fast and so on. The other reason is that we focus too much on the mechanics of the fast. The focal point of fasting deals with the condition of the heart; the focus should never be on the actual mechanics of fasting.

Jesus both taught and modeled fasting. In the book of **St. Matthew 4:2**, the Bible says that Jesus was led into the wilderness where he fasted 40 days and 40 nights. When He emerged from the wilderness, He did so with power and authority and began the work that God assigned to His hands.

So one of the purposes for fasting is to prepare us for ministry. This does not necessarily refer to preaching, but I'm talking about being prepared for whatever God has charged us to do. When we fast, we are in effect crucifying this flesh and as the physical man is diminishing, the spiritual man is being strengthened, renewed and equipped for the service of the Lord. Fasting makes us receptive to the operation of the Holy Spirit.

Another purpose for fasting is to break the strong holds of the enemy. Remember the incident in the book of **St. Mark 9**? A man brought his son who was vexed with a dumb spirit to the disciples and they could not cast out the spirit. When the father brought the son to Jesus, Jesus asked the man how long had the son been in that condition. The father answered that he'd been that way since childhood. After Jesus cast out the demonic spirit, the disciples asked Him privately why couldn't they cast the spirit out and Jesus answered and said, *"This kind can come forth by nothing, but by prayer and fasting."*

There are some long-standing, tired, stubborn issues in our lives where the enemy has constructed and erected strong holds and it is going to take an anointing that can only come through turning that plate over!

God will show us our true spiritual condition through fasting. When we fast, we become sensitive to the things of God. We began to discern and identify aspects of our lives that are not aligning with the word of God. It is only then that we can confront and correct those negative behaviors and habits, and gain strength as we bring our bodies under subjection to the authority and the will of God.

When we combine fasting, with getting on our face before God and praying and opening his word, we will experience a heightened awareness of the spiritual realm and the things of God.

Chapter 20

COMPASSION

Compassion

The Spirit of the Lord is upon Me, because He hath anointed Me to preach the gospel to the poor; He hath sent Me to heal the brokenhearted, to preach deliverance to the captives, and recovering of sight to the blind, to set at liberty them that are bruised.
(St. Luke 4:18)

Compassion is defined as a deep awareness of and empathy for another's suffering combined with a desire to alleviate or reduce that suffering. The operative word in that definition is *combined.* Because it is not enough to feel empathetic, but that empathy must be coupled with action. Jesus met the physical, the emotional, and the spiritual needs of the people. He not only saved their souls, but He healed their bodies, He fed them with meat and bread, and He ministered to their emotionally, wounded spirits.

One day my son came home from work obviously concerned about something. My son is the kind of person who is laid back and not easily shaken, but I could tell that something was wrong from the way that he came into the house and immediately came into my room. He began to share with me concerning a young lady on his job who had a niece who was very ill and had been hospitalized.

The young lady told him that her niece was in intensive care with a very extensive infection. It seems that the little girl, who was 10 years old, had been playing and broke or fractured one of her legs. A cast was placed on the leg, and after a while, she began to complain that the leg was hurting.

The little girl was taken to the hospital, and upon removing the cast, the Doctor discovered that the skin on her leg literally pulled away with the cast. Also he could see that a very progressive infection has spread throughout her leg.

Consequently, she fell into a semi-coma and even though antibiotics were administered, she was given only a 50/50 chance of survival. They were also considering amputating one of her legs. This little girl was only 10 years old!

My son said to me, "Mama, I want to do something, but I feel so helpless." He asked if we had any blessed oil. I gave my son the blessed oil and I began to pray for the little girl, planning to visit her as soon as I had all the information regarding the name of the hospital, room number, etc. In the interim, I told him to give the blessed oil to her aunt so that she could take it to the hospital and anoint her niece. Neither my son nor I knew at this point exactly where she was hospitalized. I asked him to get the information from the aunt. The next day, he obtained the information and we went to see her.

When we got to the information desk to obtain visitors passes, we were told that the little girl had been moved from intensive care to a regular room. I had mixed feelings about that information because I did not know if they had amputated her leg, or if she was still in a coma or exactly what to expect once we got to her room.

When we arrived to the room, we were greeted by the little girl's mother whom we had never met. She looked at us very suspiciously, but after introducing ourselves, we were allowed to enter the room.

We saw a little girl lying down watching television. She was wrapped in a blanket and other than looking a little weak, she seemed fine.

I finally asked the hard question about the amputation. When she lifted the blanket, I could see that both legs were intact. I said to her, "Honey, God healed you." I told her mother the same thing. Her mother acknowledged that it must have been God because the doctors had all but given up on her.

I was told that when she was in the coma, she was placed on a ventilator and had been fed through a feeding tube. While I was there, a dinner tray was brought into the room. When my son and I left, she was sitting up in her bed, talking to her mother, and eating a hamburger and french fries. Glory to God!

Why am I telling you this story? Because the real work is out there. It is not always behind a pulpit, or behind a podium, or behind a microphone.

The Lord demonstrated to me in a dream exactly what it means to show compassion. In the dream, I was standing behind the podium delivering a message. As I was teaching, a woman who needed deliverance came up to me and stood in front of the podium. I stood there for a moment, debating whether or not I should continue the message and let the deacons or someone else handle it, or leave the podium and minister to this woman. I was leaning toward ignoring the woman. After all (I reasoned) the service must go on and I must remain within the constraints of the schedule. How dare I leave the podium in the middle of teaching to minister to this woman. And wasn't I ministering already? What about protocol?

In the dream, I felt the anointing of God as He moved upon me to abandon the podium and go and minister to this woman.

What did the dream mean? It doesn't take the gift of discernment or the gift of interpretation to know that the dream was about priorities. I'm not suggesting that we should abandon the pulpit and disband the Bible classes. But what I am saying is that the bottom line is showing compassion.

I remember watching a religious program one evening. An Evangelist was speaking to his congregation and he asked them, "How many conversations have you had on this week?" And many of them began to tell him about conversations with their families, and other people. He then asked the question, "How many people have you talked to about the salvation of their souls?" A hush fell over the crowd. One woman who was obviously, visibly convicted began to weep openly.

It is a very sobering thought when we realize that every person who we encounter, whether they are members of our own family or whether they are rank strangers, have one of two conditions: They are either saved or they are lost. There is no middle ground and there are no grey areas where salvation is concerned! Only two conditions: They are *saved* or they are *lost*. And if they are lost, our position and our responsibility is clear.

Chapter 21

FORGIVENESS

Forgiveness

And be ye kind one to another, tenderhearted, forgiving one another, even as God for Christ's sake hath forgiven you. ***(Ephesians 4:32)***

When we want to get our physical bodies in shape, we refrain from eating unhealthy foods and replace them with healthy nutrients. We have learned that when our natural bodies become toxic, our entire system becomes extremely compromised. Impurities that are not properly eliminated, adversely affect every cell in our bodies.

We can apply this same principle to our spiritual man. Is it possible that our inner man can become toxic? If that is true, then it is time for Spiritual Detoxification. We can begin this process of Spiritual Detox by beginning with a very basic and fundamental principle: Forgiveness.

I once heard a preacher say that there is a scripture in the Bible that has greater consequences than perhaps that of any other passage. It is found in the book of **St. Matthew 6:12,14, 15**. And it says this: *"And forgive us our debts, as we forgive our debtors. For if ye forgive men their trespasses, your heavenly Father will also forgive you. But if ye forgive not men their trespasses, neither will your Father forgive you your trespasses."*

The implication of that passage is that God is going to relate to us in the same manner in which we relate to one another. The Bible conceptualizes forgiveness as "passing on to those who have sinned against us the mercy that we ourselves received from God." In other words, we must extend to others the same grace that we received from God. And there must be a distinction and a difference between how we as believers respond and how the world responds. If there is no difference in the response, then there should be no difference in the consequences!

Forgiveness is a major theme throughout the entire Bible. We see it in the story of Joseph and his brothers; the Prodigal Son and his father; and David and Saul. Most importantly, we see it demonstrated at Calvary when Jesus was hanging on the cross. We have no record in the Bible where the soldiers standing at the foot of the cross asked Jesus for forgiveness; No one said to Him "Forgive us from beating you, spitting on you, stabbing you and nailing you to the cross." But Jesus, with His dying breath said, *"Father, forgive them for they know not what they do."*

I feel very strongly that as the people of God, we need to be exposed to the message of forgiveness because unforgiveness is one of the weapons that the enemy uses to keep us bound, to keep us from moving forward, and to hinder the flow of the anointing.

Although we may emerge from trials, tests, and negative situations with some level of success, quite often there are some residual effects. Could it be that we have not released the disappointment, the hurt, or the frustration? Or could it be that we have not released the *person* who has caused the disappointment, the hurt, or the frustration? Pain, resentment, and bitterness of the past can erode our present as well as our future.

It is not my intent to minimize the effects of the offense. If I were to talk to everyone who is reading this book, there would be a story. And I could certainly add some stories of my own. We've all been hurt! We've all been disappointed! Most of us have been rejected at some point in our lives. Things that we encounter in life sometimes just leave our insides hurting. However, if we could just embrace the concept of forgiveness, it would liberating!

I believe that most of us are under the impression that if we release offenders, we will be required to remain in toxic relationships or that we may be opening the door for further infractions.

I don't think that most of us realize that we can establish and maintain healthy boundaries even after forgiveness because we equate forgiveness with being held in the same position. We don't realize that releasing the person who may have offended us will propel us into those new opportunities and into new relationships. However, if we do not forgive, that bitterness will bleed into that new relationship and those new opportunities.

We have focused on what forgiveness *is*; now let us focus on what forgiveness *is not***.** Forgiveness is not approval for what a person did. God never approved of our sin and He never endorses or condones our sin. If you stole from me, then you stole. If you lied on me, then you lied.

Forgiveness is not explaining away inappropriate behavior nor is it justifying what was done. In other words, forgiveness is not releasing a person from the consequences of his or her actions. If an individual committed a heinous crime, that individual *should* go to jail.

Forgiveness does not mean that what was done is forgotten; memory is a protection mechanism that God gives us. Memory is what prompts us to repeat positive experiences. But at the same time, it helps us to avoid those experiences that were not pleasant. If an individual purposely offends me every time we interact, I need to remember that so that I can avoid those kinds of encounters with that particular individual. However, just because we can recall what was done, does not mean that we ever have the right to penalize anyone for it. We must leave that to God.

So how do we forgive? First of all, we must keep in mind that forgiveness does not always result in reconciliation. In fact, forgiveness has nothing to do with the other person at all! Forgiveness has nothing to do with the person who offended us coming back and asking us to forgive them. That might not *ever* happen! Forgiveness begins with us. It begins with a decision and not a feeling. The decision to forgive is not predicated on whether or not the issues have been resolved, the relationship has been restored, or the parties have reconciled.

To recap: Forgiveness does not involve approval for what was done, the dismissal or explaining away of inappropriate behavior, or rescuing the offender from the consequences of wrong actions. Forgiveness does not require that we remain in toxic relationships or that we leave the door open for further infractions. We can establish and maintain healthy boundaries even after forgiveness.

Chapter 22

LOVE

Love

Love is patient, love is kind. It does not envy, it does not boast, it is not proud. It does not dishonor others, it is not self-seeking, it is not easily angered, it keeps no record of wrongs. Love does not delight in evil but rejoices with the truth. It always protects, always trusts, always hopes, always perseveres.
(I Corinthians 13:4-7) (NIV)

Approximately ten years ago, our city suffered several severe storms. Out of the 2.4 million customers that our local electric company serves, statistics say that approximately 1 million lost power. The storms toppled buildings, street lights, and hundreds of trees.[9]

The damage was so great, that our city solicited assistance from the surrounding communities of Illinois and as far away as Arkansas, Indiana, Iowa, Kansas, Kentucky, Louisiana, Michigan, Mississippi, Oklahoma, Tennessee and Texas.

As devastating as the storms were, I saw something beautiful occurring all over our city; as soon as one individual's power was restored, that individual would open their homes to others who had no power. In my immediate neighborhood, there was a lady who opened up her entire home to people who had not had their power restored. I was brought to tears as I saw people lined up at her door, waiting to go into her home. Some were in wheelchairs and others were only capable of mobility through the assistance of walkers.

There was a moment in space when we forgot about to whom we were not speaking and we began to inquire about the well being of others. We called to check on our relatives and friends; we shared our fans, our batteries, our food, and our water. Some of us even washed clothes for those who had not had their power restored and could not operate their washer and/or dryer.

We found out what it truly meant to have an empty refrigerator because we had to discard all of our food that had turned rancid due to the lack of refrigeration. We had to resort to boiling water if there was no bottled water on hand. We discovered that money wasn't everything because those of us who had money, could not spend it. We had money, but the hotels were full and we could not reserve a room. We had money, but there was no meat available to buy. We had money, but the gas stations and the restaurants were closed.

In short, we were all reduced to a common level. In the absence of the radio, the television, and the internet, we were forced to talk to one another. With little or no distractions, we had time to think and reflect on all those things that we had taken for granted. We were humbled and our hearts were made tender.

Concern and love were demonstrated on a level that we had not experienced in a long time.

Someone wrote a song that asked the question, "What's love got to do with it?" The answer to that question is *everything*! Love has *everything* to do with *everything*.

Paul gives love as the short answer to all of the questions and issues that the Corinthian church faced during the time that he wrote the letter to the church at Corinth.

Paul was simply saying that if love is not driving everything that we do; if love is not at the center of everything that we do; and if love is not the motivating force behind everything that we do, then whatever we are doing is just an empty mechanical, methodical gesture. Love puts everything into proper perspective.

Love has many meanings in the English Dictionary. It can describe an intense feeling of affection, an emotion or an emotional state. It can describe everything from an emotion that gives pleasure to an emotion that demonstrates patriotism.

Someone one once said, "My only regret is that I have but one life to give to my country." The sentiment is heroic, but the reality is that though I give my body to be burned and have not love, it profits me nothing.

We live in a culture today where the word *love* is bantered about so often and so casually that it has become virtually meaningless. We say that we love cake, and we love ice cream, and we love to travel, and we love a good sale.

The verses of scripture at the beginning of this chapter let us know what the characteristics of love are. That passage clarifies that love is more than a feeling or an emotion.

Most importantly, love keeps no record of wrongs. I sometimes hear Christians pray, "Lord avenge me of my adversaries!" I'm not altogether convinced that we should pray that prayer because in essence we are saying, "God, get 'em!" Instead, we may want to pray for God to have mercy because when God starts meting out punishment and exacting judgment, chances are He's going to go straight down the line just as He did in the Garden of Eden. Remember? He dealt with Adam, Eve, *and* the serpent. So we may find ourselves standing in that line because of what we may have on *our* hands.

God's way is the way of love because God is the initiator of love. God *IS* love! When God gave us His son, His love entered and embraced a sin sick world. When we love, we are simply duplicating and extending the love that God demonstrated toward us. He first loved us and He loves us with an everlasting love!

The Characteristics of Love

Love Is Long-Suffering
Love patiently waits and attempts to win over the other person even if it is our enemy.

Love Is Kind
Kindness includes attributes like friendliness, compassion, generosity, and tenderness.

Love Is Not Jealous
Jealousy is a feeling of displeasure caused by the prosperity of another, coupled with a desire to wrest the advantage from the person who is the object of one's envy.

Love Vaunts Not Itself
Love seeks to extol the virtues of others. Love has words of encouragement for the lonely, the down-trodden, and others who need uplifting.

Love Is Not Puffed Up
The original language here denotes one who is inflated with a sense of personal pride.

Love Does Not Behave Itself Unseemly
Love doesn't deliberately seek to be offensive.

Love Seeks Not Its Own
Love does not pursue its own interests. Love is not selfish.

Love Is Not Quickly Provoked

Love is slow to anger and is not overly sensitive.

Love Takes No Account of Evil

Love does not keep score.

Love Does Not Rejoice in Unrighteousness, But Rejoices with the Truth

Since love always seeks the good of others, it can never rejoice when evil prevails. When a brother or sister falls, we should never entertain secret thoughts of satisfaction. Rejoicing in the downfall of others is at variance with Biblical love.

Love Bears All Things, Believes, Hopes, and Endures

Love supports, uplifts, and undergirds those who are in need of encouragement. Love is optimistic; it entertains the highest expectations.

If we must err on the pessimism/optimism scale, let us err in the direction of hope. Even when adversity challenges again and again, love continues to prevail. True love does not give up—on God, on ourselves or on others.[10]

Notes

Chapter 3

1. **Edwin C. Bass**. "*The Empowered Church Declaration.*" Edwin C. Bass Ministries. (2009).

Chapter 4

2. **Mel Gibson.** "*The Passion of the Christ.*" A Biblical drama starring Jim Caviezel as Jesus Christ. (2004).

Chapter 5

3. **Alan Carr.** "*Watchman, What of the Night?*" (2003).

Chapter 6

4. **Virtues for Life.** "*Which Wolf Will You Feed?*" A Native American Indian Folklore. (2010-2015).

Chapter 7

5. **David Humpal.** "*The Importance of God's Word: Help for the Hurting Christian.*" (n.d.).

Chapter 12

6. **Myrtle L. Humphrey.** "*How Spiritual Warfare Sets the Captives Free.*" A Workshop. (2015).

Chapter 17

7. **Rosetta Watts, D.D.** "*The Promise, The Purpose, and The Power of The Holy Spirit.*" A Sermon. (circa 1980).

Chapter 18

8. **Dele Oke.** "*Different Types of Prayer.*" (2009).

Chapter 22

9. **The Associated Press**. "*Massive Blackout Continues in St. Louis.*" (2007).

10. **Dianne Pomon**. "*The Love Chapter.*" (2000).

Made in the USA
San Bernardino, CA
12 June 2015